MIRACLES OF
SAI
Forever & Beyond

DWARKAMAI - A MAGICAL TRIP
by Sujay Khandelwal

Readers Opinion...

After reading this delightful book in a single sitting, I have to say it is now a permanent fixture on my bedside right next to the Sri Sai Satcharita. The author has managed to capture such raw emotions experienced to people of Baba's faith. His calling was my calling, his journey was my journey, Baba's call to him was Baba's call to me. Thank you for writing this booking and sharing it with us.

- MS
A wonderful book that brought tears to my eyes

A short trip to Shirdi is enriched by Baba's miracles which make for fascinating reading. Written with pure love and Bhakti bhav, the book makes a very good reading and is a good source of Sai mahima. It serves well to instil and strengthen Faith. Lucid language helps a focused reading. A book every Sai devotee and every person whom Baba has brought to His fold must read.

- Bindu Midha
Miracle Trip

A very engrossing narrative of the author's divine experiences at Shirdi. Most Sai devotees would have experienced these at some point of time. No wonder each one of us feel he is 'Mere Sai'. The book is in simple language, keeps the reader's attention in tact and easily relatable by all Sai devotees. A real gift to every Sai lover which will kindle their own memories of similar experiences.

- Mala Mani
Everyone's Mere Sai

MIRACLES OF
SAI
Forever & Beyond

SUJAY KHANDELWAL

ARATHI NAGESH

STERLING

STERLING PUBLISHERS (P) LTD.
Regd. Office: A1/256 Safdarjung Enclave, New Delhi-110029.
CIN: U22110DL1964PTC211907
Phone: +91 82877 98380/ +91 120-6251823
e-mail: mail@sterlingpublishers.in
www.sterlingpublishers.in

Miracles of Sai – Forever & Beyond...
© 2023, Sujay Khandelwal
ISBN 978-93-93853-41-7

All rights are reserved.
No part of this publication may be reproduced, stored in a retrieval system or transmitted, in any form or by any means, mechanical, photocopying, recording or otherwise, without prior written permission of the original publisher.

Printed and Published by

Sterling Publishers Pvt. Ltd.,
Plot No. 13, Ecotech-III, Greater Noida - 201306,
Uttar Pradesh, India

Contents

Preface		*vii*
Foreword-1 – by Rakesh Juneja		*xi*
Foreword-2 – by Amulya Ratna Nanda		*xiii*
Introduction-1 – by Sujay Khandelwal		*xv*
Introduction-2 – by Arathi Nagesh		*xxiv*
1.	Dwarkamai – A Magical Morning	1
2.	I look at you - You look at me	9
3.	Sai – Brings Back Life	13
4.	Climax of a Jwellery Box	21
5.	Sai Baba and Us: Meeting Sai Baba the very first time	27
6.	Be Careful - Roopa	33
7.	Sai Ghar	39
8.	Kripa on Roopa	42
9.	A Life Saved	50
10.	Shirdi's Soil Heals	54
11.	Queue Reschedulled	59
12.	Sai Brings Back Hope	67
13.	Sai The Savior	72

14.	Close Doors Opened	76
15.	My Naughty Boy - My Sai	80
16.	9 Packets of Udi	89
17.	Baba Accepted Dakshina	95
18.	Quench for Darshan	99
19.	Miraculous Debt Recovery	102
20.	Deal blessed by Baba	106
21.	Sai removes hurdles	109
22.	Sai-Maa	113
23.	Seperation averted	116
24.	Corona Cured	125
25.	Miracle of 9 weeks Vrat	131
26.	Healing Journey	135
27.	Connect Directly – Said Sai	139
28.	Universal Sai	144
29.	Faith Instilled	157
30.	Lamp of Faith	161
31.	And Mama Returned	165
32.	Rekha's Nightmare Averted	169
33.	Baba Main Jaaoon?	174
34.	Birth of Shraddha	184
35.	The Poster Competition	189
36.	Sai Leela with Jayshree	192

PREFACE

There are many such persons, whose desire for Baba's darshan was not thus satisfied. If these persons, believing in Him, listen to His Leelas, their quest for milk (darshan) will be, to a great extent, satisfied by the butter-milk (Leelas). Chapter XII-Shri Sai Satcharita

Deep love and gratitude towards the kindest Saint in this world Shri Sainath Maharaj who inspired both the authors – *Ms. Aarthi Nagesh* and *Mr. Sujay Khandelwal* to take this endeavor of bringing forth the Miracles of Sai for the welfare of his devotees and humanity at large. Sai Baba, God incarnate took Avtar to spread love and humanity in masses. His grace looms as Miracles to ordinary people which heals their souls.

Aarthi and Sujay are ardent devotees of Sai Baba and in their lives have faced enough miracles by their beloved Lord Sai that they decided on their very first meeting only to bring to world the splendid leelas of

Baba – Miracles – in form of a book for quenching the thirst of all Sai lovers. With the firm faith that Miracles of Sai will last till the end of this world. The authors wish that the book is incessant as remembrance of His Leelas is only way to happiness, peace and salvation.

With these noble intentions in heart and blessings of Lord Ganesh they started this humble effort of bringing out to you wonderfully blissful Leelas – Miracles of Sai Baba from various corners of this world. They assimilated various miraculous experiences and incidents that devotees have faced across the globe and gave it words in the shape of a book. Both feel highly indebted and thankful to the merciful Baba who only planted this idea of collecting and editing His Miracles in their hearts and mind.

For an author it is much easier to pen down his/her own experiences, but to compile and write another devotee's experience is not an easy task. Each story has been collected from the devotee in word or voice note format and then the authors spoke to individual devotee to know more about the experiences and then the final story was written without distorting the facts. The authors have also tried to relate the stories of these devotees with the masterpiece Shri Sai Satcharita mentioning relevance of chapter numbers to which the readers can refer to. A challenge which the authors faced was how to sequence the stories.

Preface

Sai Baba himself gave the idea to do a lucky draw to sequence the stories so that there is no partiality to any devotee. Apart from first 2 stories all have gone through this process. Readers, we hope will enjoy reading each and every story which is no less than a blessing of Sainath Maharaj.

We intend to publish more stories from time to time in future. Authors will not live forever, but the book shouldn't stop releasing ever is the intent of both the authors. Sai Baba is such a Guru who keeps stunning his devotee's by showing them miracles. The authors have experienced so many miracles in their life which have brought about a change in their lives to trust and believe in Sai with complete surrender backed by unconditional Faith. A few things which are common between both the authors are that they have unshakable Faith in Sai, they Love Sai, they love to speak about Sai, they keep feeling the blessings of Sai, they try to learn more about Sai and live each moment with Sai.

FOREWORD - 1

The Wondrous Fakir of Shirdi, who has performed endless Leelas during His lifetime and the legacy of His Leelas is continuing even after 100 years of His Mahasamadhi. This makes us realise that He has not gone anywhere and is present among all of us in a *Nirakaar* form (without any form) and showing His immense love, Grace and Blessings, which the stories of this book clearly depicts.

His miraculous words that he will continue divine Karma even though he leaves human body, this fact is emerging true and the same has been noticed and experienced by many devotees around the world. The book *Miracle of Sai Forever and Beyond* looks to be an excellent endeavour that reveals some heart throbbing experiences that devotees came across in their lives which gradually increased faith in Sai Baba and his omnipresence is established time and again.

There have been thousands of books written on Sai Baba in the past, which makes us believe that the simple looking Fakir was not only a Saint but God's incarnation in this *Kaliyuga* (materialistic world). Devotees feel and experience Him as a living God on Earth showering Godly Grace for welfare of all living beings including plants and animals.

Devotees find His presence in their day-to-day life. Sai Baba attracted devotees from around the world to come to Shirdi and He blessed them by fulfilling their worthy materialistic and Spiritual desires thereby, devotees feel that there is someone to take care of them, who is listening to their compassionate prayers and fullfiling them too.

I Congratulate, Shri Sujay Khandelwal and his co-writer Smt. Aarthi Nagesh and the entire team who have made great efforts to collect and write the marvelous divine experiences of devotees and have made incredible efforts to publish the book on Sai Baba.

The book is well written with some amazing experience of devotees across the globe and I am sure it will inspire Shraddha (Faith) & Saburi (Patience) in devotees.

I will also like to appreciate Shri Surinder Ghai (President of Sterling Publishers) who has published more than 100 books on Baba for past three decades and spreading blessings to devotees all around the Globe. This book is one more milestone in his praiseworthy devotional journey.

My best wishes and prayers for the enormous success of the book.

Jai Sairam

Rakesh Juneja
(Sai Gyaneshwari)

FOREWORD - 2

I had the opportunity to go through the manuscript of the book *Miracles of Sai, Forever and Beyond* authored by Shri Sujay Khandelwal and Smt. Aarthi Nagesh. I find the book very innovative and interesting. The wide canvas of narrations of Sai devotees, both in terms of geographical locations in India and abroad, as well as themes is a unique feature of the publication.

Connecting each story with some Sai Vaani with reference to Shree Sai Satcharita is a very innovative feature.

Narrating personal mystical or miraculous experience around the unique mystic Saint and Sadguru Shirdi Sai (with the devine attributes of omniscience, omnipresence and omnipotence) needs to be attempted in a very responsible, ethical and truthful manner (For example Dabholkar, B V Narsimha Swami, Rigopoulos, Marianne Warren, Sai Saran Anand, and CB Satpathy). This being basically a collection volume the role of the two authors is extremely crucial in this context.

I pray Sadguru Sai to bless both the authors, all the narrators and publisher so that they continue to follow the Shirdi path of Shraddha and Saburi, Sadguru *samarpan*, selfless service and *Sach* (truth) in future and share such personal experiences which appears miraculous and mystical.

Jai Shri Sai

Amulya Ratna Nanda
(*Author of* : The Eternal Sai Phenomenon,
The Eternal Sai Consciousness,
The Mystery Saint of Shirdi &
The Shirdi Path to Happiness)

New Delhi

INTRODUCTION - 1

Variety in Upadesh

- *After performing many deeds of merit, you are born as a man, and if you act like this, will Shirdi help you in any way? Needless to say, that the Bhakta took the lesson to his heart, and went away.*

- *If any devotee meditated on Him day and night with complete self-surrender, he experienced complete union (without any difference) with Him like sweetness and sugar, waves and sea, eye and its sight.*

- *He gave in person or by vision and dream to one addicted to drink, He appeared in his dream, sat on his chest, pressed it and left him, after he gave a promise not to touch liquor anymore. Chapter XVIII and XIX – Shri Sai Satcharita*

Every breath I breathe nowadays is by the grace and mercy of my Sai. His omnipresence stuns me often. He answers all my questions so patiently and at times I have one to one conversation which are mostly initiated by me and sometimes by HIM. He converses with me mostly like a friend, but He guides me more like my father, my mother and my Guru. He is one with whom I can share anything and everything. I do not feel any guilt when I confess to him about my mistakes or shortcomings.

I am a human being who has been brought up in such a religious and spiritual environment where worship of God has been injected into me from the childhood. Even today when I look back at my childhood, it reflects in the Shivling (idol) of Lord Shiva which my father bought me even before my teens as I kept insisting and persuaded him. I do not know how and when that pooja turned into devotion in my life. My life journey of 47 years now has seen phases when I dropped out God from myself and then again held him back or rather, I would say He held me back to make me believe in Him. It's not been a normal life like any other individual that I have spent in these years until Sai shook me completely to make me believe in him unconditionally.

Like most of the Hindu families I too have been introduced by my family to the common gods, Lord

Rama, Krishna, Shiva, Durga, Kali etc. but it was my wife Mrs. Riya Khandelwal on whom I have my highest gratitude to connect me to my Guru who is *Anant Koti, Brahmandanayak, Rajadhiraj, Yogiraj, Parabrahma, Shree Sachidanand Sadguru Sainath Maharaj*. During our courtship period my wife who is such a staunch devotee of Sai, took me once to the Sai mandir near her house in Kolkata. Those days I was going through a phase where in God for me was just to do a mandatory Pooja, as not doing that would bring about an unrest in my mother's heart. My first visit to Sai mandir in 1998 stunned me as I saw the pictures of the gods of Hindu, Muslim, Sikh and Christian together in that mandir. My mind was perplexed with so many thoughts which arose out of this unusuality. I had never ever seen such a conglomerate of gods of so many religions together in one religious place endorsing Baba's preaching of *Sabka Malik Ek*. It was thereafter I did not relent on going to that mandir whenever I was asked to. I never ever used to take the initiative though during those days.

Our marriage got fixed in the year 1999 and the wedding card was to be presented to Sai. It's a common belief in India that the first wedding invitation card goes to gods and goddesses and thus it happened in our case too. This was followed by visits to seek blessings on special occasions until it became a kind of regular affair for me. I still cannot remember how and when exactly Sai pulled me towards Him. His aura simply attracted me. I have learnt one thing from my first Guru, my Father Late Shri Shiv Shanker Khandelwal which was do not go to mandir to ask for material gains. Do not keep pleading for any object to God again and again. Just seek for his blessings. This golden rule which I learnt from my father is something which I apply daily in my life. I seldom pray to Him to seek anything in particular. The golden words which I repeat every time I prostrate to Baba is -

Daya Karo Hey Dayalu Bhagwan
Sharan Tumhari Hum Aa Pare Hai

My Kind God please shower Your kindness
as now I am in your shelter

It was after 2010 when I was in such a phase of my life when my life was not running on my own will. It was driven by the force of alcohol which made me feel dejected and my life was peeling off towards an end. The more I tried to hold on to stop this depletion the more steadfast was the progress towards destruction all around. Those days when I look back make me feel as if I was in a volcanic zone where earthquakes keep shaking you often. The floor underneath was moving away tearing me off completely to sink into darkness. The more I resisted the bigger was the next jolt. It's Sai Samarth who was holding me all those years of my life when there wasn't floor underneath and I was crippling to move on falling every now and then. In those days of utmost despair, I used to curse Sai with my crippled thoughts.

> Why me Sai?
> I love you so much Sai.
> I believe in you Sai.
> I need help from you Sai.
> Do not do this to me Sai.

Those days with each passing day both my alcohol intake and prayers increased. Seldom used to be a day when I would be late for Kakkad aarti at the South Kolkata mandir at 6.40 am. Unlike Shirdi here the aarti starts a bit late. Kakkad aarti is one such beautiful aarti which I love the most. Its longest one which continues for over half an hour and has soulful bhajans incorporated in it which touches the soul of any devotee. For years on end, I used to attend aarti and hence a time came when a book was no more required to sing along the aarti. I used to have tears along with prayers to Baba, seeking help to stop alcohol as I was unable to do that myself.

During those days my prayers had come to such a state of affairs which were self-seeking and backed by ego. I was looking out for returns of my bhakti (devotion). I was constantly asking Him to make me sober. He made me realize this golden rule.

Faith without action is dead

Sai always plays so silently in his ways which I learnt now. His plans and ways are wondrous. He takes away when he wants to give more/better. Sai has explained this to us through Shri Sai Satcharita (written by Dabholkar) that *Whatever I take from anyone I have to return it back 10 times.* From 2010 to 2018 which was the most trying period of my life, I had lost everything which I had gained in my life (Finance, Respect, Relationship, Love, Devotion, Belief, Self-confidence etc.), but Sai gave back almost everything abundantly except a few which I know He will give back someday. May these words of Sai nest in the minds of all Sai devotees for lifetime to keep Saburi (Patience) and not lose Shraddha (Faith) in Lord Sai.

He was holding me in His arms all these years of utter despair which I understood now when He miraculously marked a difference in my life through a transformation when pains and joys are no more a basis to believe or love Him anymore. Devotion cannot be shaken in any circumstances based on worldly affairs if its real. It's My Sai who brought back my faith or rather I would put it in another way,

He instilled in me his 2 basic virtues *Shraddha and Saburi* (Faith and Patience).

In 2018 Sai gave me a new life altogether with so many miracles happening now daily in my life. I wasn't an author, Sai made me one and my first book on a wondrous trip to Shirdi was published in 2021 in the name of *'Dwarkamai- A Magical Trip'* which has been blessed with so many appreciations by the devotees. By Baba's grace this has a Best Seller label also from Amazon. I am grateful to Sterling Publishers to take out its second edition in 2022 and listing it on Flipkart also in both English and Hindi versions. Moreover, now it's available internationally also in many countries, thanks to Sterling.

I was such a shy person who would never speak amongst private gatherings, forget about public, but with Baba's blessings I can stand up now and speak spontaneously on any platform. Baba inspired me and on His insist I started with a 'YouTube channel' to propagate about Sai, so that the entire world knows about my merciful Sai and seek His blessings. The channel is in the name of *'Miracles of Sai with Sujay Khandelwal'* which is growing with more and more devotees joining in and volunteering to share their miraculous stories. The best part of this channel is that neither me nor the devotee whom I interview rehearse and I mostly do not know the devotee, forget about his/her miraculous story. It's shot live and then edited and presented to devotees every Thursday.

In 2021 by the blessings of Sai, I opened up a rehabilitation center called *'Saburi Rehabilitation Center'* located in the city of Kolkata to serve the society to fight against Alcoholism and Addiction (substance use disorder). This project is a wing of our NGO, Shiv Chandra Charitable Trust which has been named after my father, Late Sri Shiv Shanker Khandelwal and my mother Chandra Prabha Khandelwal. In the past 2 years we have treated many affected people of the society who once had lost hope in their lives and are now living happily.

Before I wrap up my introduction I would like to convey my gratitude on Sainath Maharaj for inspiring me Himself to write this book, Arathi Nagesh ji for joining me as co-author of this book, B.K. Raghuprasad ji for editing this book, Deep Khemka ji for helping me in compiling the stories, Nilesh Hemani ji for helping me to select quotes from Shri Sai Satcharita, Surinder Ghai ji for publishing this book. Shri Rakesh Juneja and Shri Amulya Ratna Nanda for writing the Foreword for this book and all the devotees who have taken out time to share their stories for compiling this book. My highest gratitude always to my first guru my father Late Shiv Shanker Khandelwal ji and my mother Chandra Prabha Khandelwal ji followed by my wife Riya Khandelwal ji for connecting me to my Paramguru my Baba my God Sai and my family and friends who have showered their love during the most challenging times of my life and lastly to my both ratans (precious jewels) Smriti and Hriday.

Readers always remember what Baba said...

Mujhe sada jeevit hi jaano,
Anubhav karo satya pehchano

I am always alive,
experience the true truth of my existence

May the *Amrit* (sweet nectar) of *Bhakti* (devotion) keeps flowing in Sai devotees to reap fruits viz Self-realization, Acceptance, Surrender and Service.

Like the Kalpavriksha, may Lord Sai fulfill all His devotees desires.

Om Sai Ram

Sujay Khandelwal

Kolkata, India
Mob : (+91) 9051155503
Email : sujay@mohanimpex.com

INTRODUCTION - 2

The Taittiriya Upanishad says that Food is Brahma; from food all the creatures are born and having been born, by food they live, and after having departed, into food again they enter. When an Atithi (guest) comes to our door at noon, it is our bounden duty to welcome him by giving him food. Chapter XXXVIII- Shri Sai Satcharita

By the grace of God, blessings of my parents and my Paramguru Shri Sainath Maharaj, it feels humbling and gratifying to embark on this divine journey of journaling the experiences of the devotees of Shri Sainath Maharaj, from all over the world.

Initially when I connected for the first time with Sujay Khandelwal ji, who happens to be the main force behind this divine book, we were complete strangers. We had exchanged a few text messages, most of which were very formal and cordial. That apart, the conversation was pertaining only to Sai, with Sujay ji letting me know that he was a staunch

Sai devotee too. The next initiative he took was to bring me out on his YouTube channel and interview me on how I connected with Sainath. Dear readers, you will have to believe me when I tell you that this was the first time we saw each other, the interview flowed so seamlessly, that any viewer would get a feeling that it was rehearsed. It wasn't.... It was just Sai who was leading both of us and helped us talk. The interview covers my entire journey with Sai. But, as a co-author of this book, it is of prime importance that I capture the jist of my journey with Sai here in my introduction.

I was born in the beautiful town of Mysuru in Karnataka, in an upper middle class, cosmopolitan family. Being born as the child of a reknown professor of Mysore University, my childhood was a very secure one. I was exposed to only good things during our childhood. My dad, a writer of international fame, got home at least 3-4 books every day. Just like how we had to eat our vegetables and fruits, it was mandatory that we had to read books. This exposed us to the epics in English and our language Kannada, in very early and formative years. Back then, we did not realise its benefits, but as we grew up, we reaped rich benefits out of our upbringing. We, the three siblings, had no emotion called jealousy. The reason was simple. Though my parents claimed they had a nuclear family set up, I don't remember a single day my mom served dinner to just the five of us. We always had guests, who were welcome wholeheartedly by my parents. By the time I graduated, along with the three of us, we had three cousins and the son of a close friend completing studies in our house. I would not be exaggerating if I say, my house resembled a hostel. At one point in time, I remember my mom packing 7 lunch boxes in the morning. We grew up sharing and caring.

However, being the multilingual scholar that my dad is, he is a staunch atheist, who did not believe in the existence of God. So, worshiping a Guru was out of question. He believed in the saying 'Work Is Worship'. The many awards that he has got in state, national and international levels, stand as a testimony to this. However, this did not hamper my mother's religious activities and she would do her poojas in all grandeur. We children never sat to learn any of our prayers. We would wake up to my mother chanting Hanuman Chalisa and Shiva Panchakshari Stotra loudly. We often joked that she can serve as a lady priest and her chanting would not only wake up her household, but also the entire colony. That did not demotivate her in any way, and she would chant her morning shlokas in the same decibel the next day too!! We unknowingly knew most of these shlokas by heart. However, until I got married and saw a few ladies going to shloka classes to learn what I had learnt by listening to my mom all my childhood, I never realised the value of these early morning chanting's.

The next chapter in my life began when I got married to a workaholic husband, who was not much different than his father-in-law. He would get restless, if he would take more than a day off in a week. This attitude of him, coupled with the blessings of elders and Sainath Maharaj, has led him to be one of the most successful business leaders today. With this background introduction of mine, let us come to the most important chapter of how Baba came into my life.

Having grown up in my background, I had no exposure to Baba until 2000. I barely knew who Baba was. It was in the year 2000 that the entire world suffered a major slowdown in the business industry. Like all companies, my husband Nagesh's company also suffered the slowdown and there was a salary reduction, which was a considerable amount for those days. We were still an upcoming family, we had just had a son, bought a house and a Maruti-800 car, typical of all upcoming families. The house and the car had loans on them, and we had to pay the EMI's. That apart Nagesh, had to support his parents, as my father-in-law had no pension, and my husband was the only earning member in the family. This came as a major shock to us. The salary cut did not impact any of our day-to-day habits, we could still make both ends meet comfortably, but leading a luxurious life was out of question. Nagesh also made it clear that we may not be able to afford shopping or holidays like we used to. As a young girl, still in my early twenties, this had a huge insecurity feeling loom large over my head.

It was one such night, when I was deep asleep, a life changing dream appeared. This dream lasted for less than 30 seconds. I saw a sadhu, wearing an orange gown, with a bag hanging from his shoulder walk on a marble platform. He had tied a matching cloth covering his head. I had never seen this sadhu earlier ever and had no clue who he was. I woke up the next day reminiscing about the dream. I called up a senior colleague of my husband and shared my dream with him. Upon hearing my experience, he said 'Arathi, I think Sai Baba has appeared in your dream. Go visit his mandir when you can.' I used to go to this senior colleague, Ananta Raman for any spiritual or religious guidance. He was like an elder brother to me. That evening my husband carried home a small roll in his hand and told me that Raman had sent it and had instructed him to give it to me. I opened the rubber band that was used to tie the roll and stood in awe. Yes, this was a calendar that had the picture of the same sadhu who had appeared in my dream. The very moment I picked up the phone and called Raman and told him excitedly that it was the same sadhu I had seen in my dream. 'You are very lucky and chosen Arathi. Baba doesn't appear in the dreams of many people who have been his devotees for years. This clearly shows that you have been chosen by him. Just believe in him and see how blessed you will be' he said.

This way, Baba had entered my house and I had no clue where his blessings would take my family. I was elated and hung the calendar on the door of my cupboard. That evening, I was not the same person. There was an unexplained feeling of joy and positivity inside my house. Before going to sleep that night, I touched Baba's feet and went to sleep. This today has become my habit for the last 22 years and the only difference is, I have graduated from touching Baba's feet to talking to him every single night before I call it a day.

That night also Baba appeared in my dream. I was going on my Kinetic Honda to his mandir. I could very clearly see the number plate of my bike. I had Baba riding pillion with me and tapping my back, as if he was gesturing that 'I have your back my child…'. That dream again lasted less than 30 seconds.

By now, I knew it was time to seek his darshan and requested my close friend Anu, to take me to his mandir. She promised to take me the following Thursday. As planned, we set out to seek his darshan, the following Thursday. I was riding the same Kinetic

Honda and we were half way through when my husband called on my mobile. (Yes, I owned a mobile that early as my husband Nagesh was an employee of Motorola and was one among the first few in Bangalore to own a mobile. I got one too those days itself). To my surprise, he said there was good news and the salary roll back had happened. Not only that, the cut that was implemented, he would get that amount back as an arrears in the next salary. This experience had happened even before I took his darshan. From then, there was no going back.

Probably a month after this incident, Nagesh had to travel abroad for business purpose. Whenever he travelled, I would go and stay with one of my aunts. There were three of them who had settled in Bangalore and they would never allow me to stay with the child all alone. It was during one such evening, my uncle Mr. Ashok Mehta had taken us to the Cubbon Park in Bangalore, to get a ride in the toy train there for my son. As we sat on the bench, savoring the taste of freshly burnt sweet corn, I shared my dream and my experience with Baba that had taken place so far. My uncle also knew about Baba and a few of his relatives were devotees of Baba. He told me that evening 'Arathi, please do not ignore the fact that Baba has appeared in your dream. It means that you have got a *bulaava* (invitation) from him. It is perfectly okay that you have visited his mandir here in Bangalore but please do visit Shirdi at the earliest. Do not ignore his invitation. There are many of his devotees, that I know of, who plead with him to appear in their dreams. He doesn't give darshan that easily. Please understand that you are the chosen one'.

I had heard the same words from Raman also. I was now more than convinced that Baba had chosen me and I had to just believe in him and entrust my life to him. From that day onwards, I surrendered the responsibility of my family to Baba and completely surrendered myself at his holy feet. Today, as I stay a proof to the generosity of his blessings in terms of everything a woman can wish for, I feel it is my responsibility to help people realise their dreams and make them understand that 'HE can do anything for his devotees if U trust him.' The main qualities he expects out of his devotees is just *'SHRADDHA AND SABURI'*. My years of praying to him has made me lead a blessed life. I am surrounded by the best of my family, friends, all materialistic luxuries and a peaceful life. That however, doesn't mean my life is a bed of roses. I do face my share of challenges and problems in my life. Whenever I encounter such situations, all I blindly do is to connect with Baba. He gives me the courage and strength to fight the situation. He also leads me in a path, which I blindly follow because I believe that he is making me take that path. The last two decades of my life is dictated by Baba and I am a happy soul !

The whole intention of bringing out this journal also remains the same. Me and Sujay ji, want maximum people to benefit by trusting Baba wholeheartedly. Miracles will surely happen; he is a very approachable and simple Sadguru and his devotees can easily please him as he has no worldly desires.

Before I end my introduction, I would like to thank my Paramguru Sai for choosing me for this divine task, Shri. Sujay ji for trusting in my abilities, the publishers, my parents Dr. Pradhan Gurudutta and Seethalakshmi Pradhan, my husband Chinya Nagesh and my two eyes Nikhil and Nidhi.

I do sincerely hope the readers will enjoy reading this book, as much as we enjoyed writing it for you all.

With lots of love, light, power and positivity.

Loka Samastha Sukhino Bhavantu!

Om Sai Ram

Arathi Nagesh

Bangalore, India
Mob : (+91) 9845035448
Email : nagesharathi@gmail.com

1

DWARKAMAI
– A MAGICAL MORNING

However, oppressed and troubled one may be, as soon as he steps into the Masjid, he is on the pathway to happiness. Chapter XIII – Shri Sai Satcharita

12 February, 2022, morning around 6.30 am I was in the queue to take Baba's darshan outside Dwarkamai. It was my 4th and the final day in Shirdi as I had a late morning flight back home to Kolkata. 3 days had just passed away staying in Shirdi like a blink.

This was the first time ever that I had stayed in Shirdi for more than 2 days. During this visit I met Amitji (a distant relative) who has settled in Shirdi in the recent years. He connected me to Nanasaheb Shinde (4th generation of Laxmi Bai Shinde whom baba had given 9 coins), who took me around Shirdi and made me meet many close families of Shirdiet's who were the decedent's of then living souls who lived with Sai Baba when he was in his flesh and bones. I shot a lot of videos of them for my YouTube channel *'Miracles of Sai with Sujay Khandelwal'*. This kept me so busy that I somehow could not visit Dwarkamai. In the last 3 days, I had a deep longing to visit Dwarkamai but could not do it even once. I could only visit the Sanctum Sanctorum (Samadhi Mandir) few times for Aarti and darshan. Those days Shirdi had opened up full-fledged after the COVID-19 restrictions got completely removed and was crowded like always. This was the final day and anyhow I wanted to visit Dwarkamai.

That day I woke up in the morning and went for Kakkad aarti to the mandir. After a blissful aarti I came out of the mandir and headed towards Swami Madras hotel to meet Baba Iyer who is a close devotee of Baba for 7 decades. He had agreed to shoot a video that day morning and I did not want to miss doing that as he was a very staunch and close devotee of Sai. In the hotel I met Baba Iyer and reconfirmed about the shoot. Baba assured me that he will be coming to my hotel, where I was residing, Sun and Sand in half an hour himself for a shoot. I said in my mind

'I have 30 mins in hand so I can easily go and visit Dwarkamai'.

Happily thanking Baba, I headed towards Dwarkamai. It was a pleasant winter morning and I briskly walked towards the Dwarkamai not to lose time as I had to rush out of the hotel after the shoot to catch the flight.

Hurriedly I opened my slippers at the exit gate of Dwarkamai and joined the queue from the entry side. When I was quite close to enter Dwarkamai, security guard stopped me as I was carrying my mobile in my pocket. In haste I completely forgot to deposit my mobile at the mobile deposit counter. As the mobile deposit counter was quite far, I requested the security guard pleading that I was getting late and to allow me to go inside, assuring I won't be using the mobile inside. But my request was rejected. I had to take the darshan but time was short. I rushed out of the queue not thinking what to do next as it was pointless wasting time pleading to the security guard.

Once out of the queue, I looked opposite and saw many shops open. These shops who sell Sai's articles do open up early morning to cater to the visitors. I headed to the one just opposite to save time and requested the person sitting on the counter to keep the mobile for a while.

'Where are you going to go'? asked the shop keeper.

'I will just do a darshan and will be right back' I told him.

'But Darshan where'? asked the shopkeeper again.

'Dwarkamai' I meekly replied

He agreed to keep the mobile as he knew that I will be back soon. If I were to go to Samadhi Mandir then probably, he would not have kept my mobile as it takes longer there. I happily came out of the shop and joined the queue again. This time the queue was longer than last time. I had no choice but to rejoin if I had to take darshan. So, I joined the queue which was moving at a snail speed. I still had few minutes so I did not worry much. I murmured to myself 'Finally I will be doing the darshan'. Excited and feeling blessed I moved ahead with the queue. When I was just near to entering Dwarkamai, a voice came from nowhere

Sujay, take 7 rounds of Dwarkamai!
the voice was loud and clear.

Was it Baba?

Did I hear rightly or was it a figment of my imagination?

During this visit, I did not get much time to come to Dwarkamai in-spite of this being my longest stay ever in Shirdi in the past 20+ years. I always used to stay there for one or maximum two nights.

I understood it was Sai who instructed me to take 7 rounds. But it was impossible for me to do so as I did not have time. I said to Sai in my mind

'Sorry Sai but I shall not be able to do that. So please *Kshama* (forgive me)'.

I moved inside Dwarkamai and got lost feeling the bliss of Saimay environment there. I took the round and after I crossed the stone on which Baba used to sit, I recollected Baba's words. 'Take 7 rounds Sujay'. Confused but sure that it was not possible until I wish to miss the shoot or the flight. I started moving out and once I came out, a kind of a pull let me join the queue again. I had a similar pull in 2020 which I had mentioned in my previous book, *Dwarkamai - A Magical Trip.* I said to myself

'If Sai wants then ok, I will take 3 rounds but not more'.

I had done a deal with Sai in my mind. More than 3 rounds was impossible. So, I made up my mind to hear to Baba's advice at least little if not complete. Queue wasn't smaller than earlier but I had to do it as I had made up my mind to take 3 rounds. It took me 15 minutes to complete the second and third round. Happy and blessed I got out after the

3rd round to wear my slippers. But Sai won't let me go. Like a magnet in spite of not wanting I found myself standing in the queue again. This time I had surrendered myself. Thought of missing the shoot or the flight completely vanished from my mind. Anxiety, Fear and Hurry was all warded off and it was just the blissful feeling which prevailed. My mind was blank with no thoughts at all. It just said 'If Sai wants it let it be'. I could just feel Sai Sai and Sai...

4th round was fater than the earlier ones...

5th even faster as there were very few people

6th was the one when I just walked casually inside without a queue with very few devotees

Next was the 7th and the final round. I was constantly counting them so that I do not make a mistake. This time I walked coolly inside and to my surprise I saw just 2 devotees who were moving out of Dwarkamai. I couldn't believe this and turned all around to see who else was there. Those two devotees also moved out then.

Uncontrollable tears started flowing from my eyes. These were tears of gratitude. How Sai cleared up and made way for me so that I could do all rounds as per his instruction. I stood wonderstruck there facing the inside of Dwarkamai. Once I looked at the *Dhuni* on my left and then at Baba's picture on my right. Then straight on the wall where the garland was hanging. I stood there and spoke to Sai...

Thank You Sai !

I am sorry Sai !

I was trying to disobey your instructions without even remembering the fact that it's you who is the driving force behind my life. You have made impossible, possible in my life and this new life is just a gift from you.

Please forgive me Sai for again trying to impose My Will and not understanding Your Will.

Tears didn't stop.

I was talking to Sai.

I could see his face there on the wall clearly.

I went into a state of trance.

Suddenly I regained my consciousness to see few devotees there behind me forming a queue waiting for me to give them space for darshan. I immediately bowed down to Sai, thanked him for such a blissful darshan and said Good Bye to him and moved out of Dwarkamai happily. Nothing got delayed which I was doubting and contemplating in my mind and the shoot was done gracefully with the most humble Sai Sevak, Baba Iyer and I checked out of the hotel to take a flight and came back safely without any hitches back home.

Even today when I think of that moment, goosebumps just covers my entire body and I feel so blessed that my Paramguru, my God, my Sai Baba gave me darshan and spoke to me there in Dwarkamai.

You are my Love Sai

I love you Sai

Sujay Khandelwal

Mob : (+91) 9051155503
Email : sujay@mohanimpex.com

2

I LOOK AT YOU - YOU LOOK AT ME

'Those who are fortunate and whose demerits have vanished; take to My worship. If you always say 'Sai, Sai' I shall take you over the seven seas; believe in these words, and you will be certainly benefited. I do not need any paraphernalia of worship - either eight-fold or sixteen-fold. I rest there where there is full devotion'. Chapter XIII - Shri Sai Satcharita

It was mid 2021. The whole world was slowly recovering from the notorious pandemic. The huge bungalow in the outskirts of Bangalore was resonating with Sai bhajans since early morning. As the lady of the house, I settled down on the couch, with my filter coffee in hand. I couldn't help but wonder, 'how I wish there was a Sai mandir which was easily approachable.' My thoughts took me back to my life in Singapore. An MRT ride of 10 minutes and a drive of another 10 minutes in city bus, would lead me to the bus stop just opposite to Sai mandir in little India. I would peacefully attend the *Madhyan Aarti* (afternoon aarti), connect with my Paramguru Sainath, re-energise myself and head back home happily. I couldn't but help wonder, if going to Sai mandir was easier abroad. I was a bit disappointed and teared up and looked at my Baba. My eyes pleaded with him

'Why are you not near my house here?'.

Never in the wildest dreams did I expect what awaited me that evening. It was around dusk, that I walked out of my bungalow, to breathe in some fresh air. I was battling a splitting headache. My husband, offered to take me on a drive, so that I would feel better. Considering the fact that we lived in the outskirts of Bangalore, fresh air was never a scarce.

I hopped into the car, rather mechanically. That day being a Thursday, my husband drove the car towards a Sai mandir that nestled amidst a village. The drive would take us about 20 minutes on the highway. Realizing the car headed towards Sai mandir, I expressed my unwillingness to go. I was not carrying my wallet. Somehow, I didn't want to see my Baba with empty hands. Baba had been very generous towards me and bestowed me with all possible luxuries. I firmly believed that it was all his grace and never wanted to see him empty handed.

In agreement with my thoughts, Nagesh (my husband) changed the direction and drove on in the opposite direction of the mandir. We exited the rear entrance of their gated community. Still, uninterested where we were going, I stared into nowhere. Nagesh was enthusiastically explaining about the cleanliness of the villages that surrounded their community. Barely two mins into the drive, we heard Sai dhun coming from nowhere. The area was completely secluded, barring a few layouts that were still coming up. We wondered where the dhun was coming from. That was the only road in front of us and so we just kept going. 50 meters into the drive, we saw a newly constructed Sai mandir, barely 4-5 minutes drive from our house. This was too shocking to believe!

I had tears welling up and Nagesh was dumbfounded!

We got down from our car, as if cast by a spell and walked towards the mandir.

Baba ki beti..... Was at his feet!

Baba yet again proved that he listens to his devotees and expects nothing from them. He not only came to a place near to our house, but also made sure that I saw him empty handed that day!

In-fact I was ashamed of my thoughts, that I thought I had to see Baba only with Dakshina.

Now, I run to Baba's mandir whenever I feel like connecting with my Guru!

Again - Baba proved one needs to keep their *Shraddha* (faith) and *Saburi* (patience) intact .

Om sai ram

Arathi Nagesh

Mob : (+91) 9845035448
Email : nagesharathi@gmail.com

3

SAI – BRINGS BACK LIFE

The son of a friend of mine at Lonavala fell ill. My friend tried all possible means, physical and spiritual, but the fever would not abate. At length, he got his Guru to sit by the bedside of his son, but this too was of no avail. Hearing this, I thought.... 'What was the utility of the Guru, if he could not save my friend's son? If the Guru can't do anything for us, why should I go to Shirdi at all?' Thinking this way, I postponed my Shirdi-trip, but the inevitable must happen, and it happened in my case as follows ..... Mr. Nanasaheb Chandorkar, who was a Divisional officer, was going on tour to Bassein. From Thana he came to Dadar and was waiting for a train bound for Bassein. Meanwhile, a Bandra Local turned up. He sat in it and came to Bandra, and sent for me and took me to ask for putting off my Shirdi Trip.

The moment I touched Sai Baba's feet, I began a new lease of life. I felt myself much obliged to those, who spurred and helped me to get the darshan, and I considered them as my real relatives. Chapter II – Shri Sai Satcharita

Nirmal Kaur is a Baba's devotee residing in Delhi. Being a single mother for last 3 years now, her life hovers around her daughter, Manvi who is 12 years of age. She has known Baba for a long time through her younger sister who is a Baba's staunch devotee since 2010. But Nirmal did not know much about Baba until 2020 when she visited Shirdi for the first time with her sister. Nirmal had come to stay at her sister's place in Aurangabad when suddenly one day this trip got organised and they visited Baba at Shirdi. On the very first meeting with Baba, Nirmal got attracted towards Him but did not have any strong belief until Baba showered His blessings through his miracle to make her a staunch devotee.

September 2022, one fine morning, Nirmal woke up her daughter, Manvi, to get her ready for school and to her surprise found her body warm. On checking she realised that she was running high fever. She immediately gave her medicines and fruits and her temperature subsided and once she started feeling better, Nirmal left for her job leaving her behind to take rest. Since the time Nirmal has seperated from her husband, she has been going through a rough patch with full responsibility of Manvi's upbringing in the best affordable ways. Nirmal had taken up a job in a restaurant as senior steward which is the only means for their livelihood.

Nirmal thought that Manvi must have got fever due to stress etc but she wasn't correct. Soon once she reached her workplace, she suddenly got a call from Manvi.. 'Ma I am not feeling well. I am shivering with cold.' This brought about an unrest in Nirmal's mind. Her workplace was 30-40 minutes away from home and she wanted someone to attend her immediately. She called up her mother whose workplace was quite near and she reached in next 10 minutes. On reaching, her mother realized that Manvi's state was not good and they decided to take her to a nearby government hospital. Nirmal, extremely worried, was stuck up in work as she had to do the opening of the restaurant and no one responsible had come by then whom she could handover and leave the restaurant. Nirmal knew her responsibilities as an employee but she had more responsibilities towards her only child who was the basis of her life. She tried hard but couldn't find a way to leave immediately until finally her boss, the restaurant owner, came and she handed over to him and rushed to the hospital.

Doctor suspected that it was tonsillitis because of which she was getting fever. Though she had gone through a whole lot of Diagnostic tests but the reports were expected later. Doctor prescribed her medicine for tonsils and released her. Manvi was brought back home in the late afternoon. Medicines continued, but the fever did not subside. Instead it went up to 104°C and the whole night Nirmal sat beside her putting cold tissues on her forehead to bring down the temperature.

Next morning, when the situation was out of control, Nirmal and her mother decided to take Manvi to hospital again. They met the doctor who casually asked Nirmal to continue with medication as he couldn't diagnose anything other than tonsillitis. But the mother's heart suspected something bigger. She remembered that the test reports must be ready by then and she straight headed towards the report collection counter. To her surprise the reports stated 'Dengue'. While she was going through the reports, she got a call from doctor. 'Madam where are you and your daughter' asked doctor. 'I have just collected Manvi's test reports doctor' replied Nirmal. 'Good that you have not left the hospital yet. Manvi's test reports state that she has Dengue and her platelets have dropped drastically. Bring her to the emergency immediately without any delay' firmly instructed doctor. Manvi's heart already knew that there was something bigger than a tonsillitis and this got confirmed by the reports and doctor too. Without wasting even a single minute, she rushed with Manvi to the emergency ward and got her admitted.

Fast forward... 10 days had passed and there was no improvement in Manvi's condition inspite of medication. Infact her situation had worsened in those 10 days. Her temperature would subside when injected with paracetamol but would again come back hitting high on the thermometer. Her platelets count instead of rising up was constantly dipping daily. She would not open her eyes even most of the times. Nirmal was having sleepless nights staying 24 hours with Manvi beside her bed in the hospital. Nirmal's mother too did not go home for all these days and spent nights there in the hospital itself waiting at the lobby. Nirmal's mother had categorically said on the very 1st day that 'I will only go home when doctors give my grandchild a discharge after recovery.' She never knew then, that Manvi will have to go through so much and the treatment will be so prolonged. Both Nirmal and her mother were themselves in a very stressful state with many sleepless nights then. Nothing much was there in their hands other than trusting doctors and praying to GOD. Nirmal's mother kept crying and praying but Nirmal's eyes could not shed even a single drop as she had to give strength to her child but deep down inside she kept weeping as she could feel her sweetheart's pain.

Here in the hospital, Nirmal and her mother were praying constantly and back there her siblings were constantly praying. Her younger sister, who took her to Shirdi, was constantly praying her Sai since the day Manvi was admitted. When the situation did not improve, she started fighting with Baba like a child and told Baba.. 'I will not believe in you and do your pooja anymore, if you do not shower your blessings on my niece to recover and get her back home.' Manvi's situation was such that doctor's had given an ultimatum of 48 hours as there was no improvement. 'If Manvi does not respond to medicines and improve in next 48 hours, her life is in danger' stated the doctor.

Sai Baba ultimately listened to her sister's prayer and miracle happened. Baba took Manvi's sufferings on himself and this was shown in the Baba's picture back at Nirmal's home. Tears started flowing from Baba's eyes in the picture. All three of her siblings went to Saibaba mandir in Lodhi Road, Delhi and prayed for her speedy recovery. All of them, were wonderstruck at this leela, did not understand why tears started flowing from Baba's eyes in the picture but later realised when immediately Manvi started recovering from that day itself. All the sisters came to hospital from Lodhi Road mandir and applied UDI on her head and made her drink Baba's water.

Manvi who couldn't even open her eyes then, sat up on her bed and drank Baba's water. After drinking that she asked for a glass of Lime water. Readers, Manvi had not taken anything orally for the last 10 days and by the grace of Sai Baba, after application of UDI and drinking Baba's Holy water, she had 2 glasses of lime water. Her fever started subsiding and in 2 days her platelet counts rose up drastically. She got discharged on the 13th day and was brought back home. Before leaving the hospital Manvi said to her mother...

Mummy mujhe Shirdi jaana hai mere birthday par, Sai Baba ke paas

Mummy I want to spend my birthday in Shirdi with Sai Baba

Nirmal could not confirm her daughter then as she had a budget constraint but as we all know when Baba calls His devotee's He will makes their way. So did he do for both of them. They have already booked their tickets for Shirdi and will be there on 14 January, 2023 to celebrate Manvi's birthday with Sai Baba. Such are Baba's ways to shower HIS blessings.

Now Nirmal and her entire family has become staunch devotees of Sai Baba.

Nirmal Kaur

Delhi
Mob : (+91) 8285690824
Email : nirmalkaur.1942@gmail.com

4

CLIMAX OF A JWELLERY BOX

After saluting Baba, Shama said, 'Deva, what is this play of Yours? You first raise a storm and make us restless and then calm it down and ease us'. Baba replied 'You see mysterious is the path of action. Though I do nothing, they hold Me responsible for the actions which take place on account of Prarabdh (destiny). I am only their witness. The Lord is the sole Doer and Inspirer. He is most merciful. Neither I am God nor Master. I am His obedient servant and remember Him constantly. He, who casts aside his egoism, and thanks Him and he, who trusts Him entirely will have his shackles removed and will obtain liberation'. Chapter XXXIV– Shri Sai Satcharita

This miracle happened with Sweety who is a resident of Riyadh in the UAE. She has numerous miraculous incidents happened in her life by the grace of Saibaba and she chooses to share one with us ...

In the year 2014 Sweety used to live in UAE with her husband and son. Her husband was employed there. In September 2014 Sweety gave birth to her second son and they named him Karthikeyan. Back in India there was a marriage in their family for which her entire family were supposed to attend. The marriage was in January 2015 and they made all preparations for coming to India and attend the marriage functions. At that time her elder son was around 1 year old and younger one was only 4 months old. They had to travel from Riyadh to Mumbai and then to Raipur where her mother's house was and the marriage function.

On the day they were travelling to Mumbai, unfortunately both her son's fell ill and complained of fever and vomiting. The parents were very worried during the travel and were praying for speedy recovery of their sons. As soon as they landed at Mumbai International airport they asked for a doctor's help for their sons. But their worries were not limited to this only. Because Sweety was attending a marriage in India she had kept all her jewellery in a box which happened to be her marriage jewellery. When they were going through Customs one official seized the box of jewellery and asked her to follow him in office cabin. She was already tensed due to her son's ill health and this was like a jolt. The officer who seized the box of jewellery said that they will have to pay tax for jewellery in box.

The valuation of jewellery was around 1.5 lacs and hence they were asked to pay a tax of rupees thirty thousand. Sweety was very unhappy with this and explained to the officer that these were her own jewellery which she got in her marriage so why should she pay tax for these now. After much deliberation and argument some sense prevailed on the official and he after two hours of conversation let them go without having to pay any tax. Sweety was very hassled in these two hours and thanked Sai for helping them secure their jewellery without having to pay any tax. She moved out of the office and attended her sons.

They had to move from international terminal to domestic as their next flight would be from there. They had landed around 12 noon and by 2 pm they got clearance from customs office. They took a bus from international terminal to reach domestic t erminal where they would take next flight. While they were on the bus to domestic terminal the bus ahead of them had a picture of Sai Baba. Sweety was very happy to see it and said a silent prayer and thanked Baba for taking them out of trouble with Customs.

They reached domestic terminal, had lunch, and were waiting for boarding announcement. Suddenly they heard the flight which was supposed to take off at 5 pm was now delayed by 30 minutes. This was running salt to anyone's wound. They had gone through enough trouble all day due to illness of their children then harassment at customs officer and now didn't want any more trouble. But as they say God always has better plans for us than we can phantom and we only understand after it happens.

While they were waiting for their half an hour delayed flight Sweety suddenly noticed the same officer from Customs office. She was surprised and perplexed as what was he doing at domestic terminal whereas his duty was at International custom terminal. As soon as the officer spotted Sweety and her family, he came to them and said that he was looking for them for more than 2 hours and ultimately, he came to domestic to look for them. Both Sweety and her husband couldn't understand the reason as to why he was again looking for them and were apprehensive as this time he was accompanied by a Police officer also. Then the Custom officer broke the news to them that they had left the Box of jewellery at his office only.

In the entire hustle-bustle both of them totally forgot that they had left the jewellery box on the table of officer who was interrogating. Both Sweety and her husband almost fell from skies. They couldn't believe that in anxiety and disturbed state of mind they had forgotten the jewellery box at Customs office. The officer handed over the box of jewellery to them and took a photo to be sent to his seniors as a proof that had returned the box to its rightful owners. Meanwhile there was a boarding announcement for their onwards flight and they took the box thanked the official and proceeded to board.

On flight Sweety recalled all incidents that happened during the day and thanked Baba for his miracles as it was nothing less than the biggest surprise she had got ever. She thanked Baba for bailing her and her family out of all hassles and returning her marriage jewellery back to her which had immense sentimental value for her. It was Baba only who saved their financial loss and took care of her ailing children also ...

She actually was short of words to thank Baba for his blessings....

There will be no adequate way of thanking Baba for His infinite mercy and love. The only way is to constantly remember Him.

Om Sai Ram

Sweety Soni

Dubai
Mob : (+)971562926848
Email : sweetysony82@gmail.com

5

SAI BABA AND US: MEETING SAI BABA THE VERY FIRST TIME*

Sai Baba often said that let His man (Devotee) be at any distance, a thousand koss away from Him, he will be drawn to Shirdi like a sparrow, with a thread tied to its feet. It is always the experience of the Bhaktas that God always helps them in their search for Sadguru and other spiritual endeavours. Chapter XXVIII – Shri Sai Satcharita

Don't believe in miracles? Neither did Bindu, a Sai devotee till she experienced personally. A beautiful journey began in August 2002.

The year 2002 initiated a remarkable change in her life when she visited Shirdi for the first time. It was Sai himself who had beckoned her and her family.

* *A Chapter taken from Everyone's Sai authored by Bindu Midha published by Notion press*

Hasn't Sai Baba asserted often – *'Only those whom he summons are able to climb the stairs of Dwarkamai.'* It happened the same way with her. She had little knowledge of this revered saint of a small town in Maharashtra. What made her take the trip to Shirdi? It was a chance meeting with an absolute stranger in Delhi. He was an astrologer, and Bindu along with her family was undergoing a trying time. They had returned from abroad and were on the lookout for a job. The astrologer recommended a pooja ceremony for their son and added that they visit Sai Samadhi Mandir in Shirdi since they were in any case travelling from Delhi all the way to Maharashtra. He shared, in confidence, that Shri Sai had helped him during a very lean phase of his life. After the visit, his personal and professional life picked up. They happened to be sailing in the same boat at that time and hence decided to take his word. Hence began their journey to Maharashtra.

She wasn't too pleased about the visit to Shirdi and thought, *'How can a man be worshipped as God? God is supreme and in a much higher realm, sort of inaccessible.'* Though she showed due regard, she certainly lacked the enthusiasm that her husband showed during this visit. The darshan, was a smooth sail and since it was the month of August (rainy season), they were the only visitors present inside the temple. It was as if the temple was only for them and the pujari seated close to the idol. (Such a darshan is impossible nowadays with multitudes that throng daily, at any time, in any season).

Once in the presence of the massive idol of Sai Baba, she looked at HIM, the same query writ in her mind. She walked in and out as if she was a tourist not a follower in a holy place. Not sure if the idol had made any impact on her thoughts and beliefs, she sauntered in and out. It was months later that feelings of respect took birth. No incident, no sudden change. Transition occurred, gradually over a period. A total disinterest, gradually transformed into belief and acceptance. She felt a deep sense of inner peace and calm take over, peacefulness that had eluded for a while when her husband sought fresh employment but hadn't been successful. They felt soothed as if an elder had stroked their head and re-assured that all would be well. The pujari informed that they were visiting on a very auspicious day. It happened to be a Thursday. Till then they had no inkling what this meant or its significance. So, Baba had called them to Him on a Thursday (*guruvar*) and signaled to them to offer to him Shraddha and Saburi.

It was during their 2nd trip to the temple on that day that she sensed a change. This time tears flowed without a warning. Unabashedly, they wept. It was as if all anxieties were getting washed away. Their worries passed to him, like little kids in the presence of their loving parents. Lost children had found their mother after a long time. The serene tranquil environment soothed them with its simplicity and cleanliness. As she bowed to the saint, he was no longer the statue of a mere man, but that of a loving mother, *Sai Ma!* This was literally her first meeting with Sai. They were at ease and felt assured that their long continuing troubles would end.

The visit to Dwarkamai and seeking blessings at the Dhuni, followed by the partaking of Udi Prasad and langar (food that visitors can eat as prasad, at a minimal or zero cost) all indicative of Baba welcoming them to his fold. He has often said that till He wishes no one can step on the soil of Shirdi. How true. They have been living in Mumbai since the last decade. But, to make a trip merely once a year has become a sort of a practice. Ironically, when they were further away, they made a conscientious effort to seek Baba's darshan each year.

After this life changing darshan, they learnt of the evening aarti and eagerly awaited to join the auspicious chanting which would ease them further. Amazed at the sight of sudden appearance of hundreds of devotees at the temple gates, they felt themselves gently propelled to reach the sanctum sanctorum in the presence of this benevolent saint for a second time the same day, a Thursday. They had much to thank him for. The visit to Dwarkamai was an exhilarating experience when, they could bow and place their heads on the actual large stone that Baba would very often sit on. How could one ask for more? It was humbling to realise that a saint of his popularity and following covered himself in a simple kafni and did not seat himself on a cushioned throne of gold or silver but a hard surface. Other items of daily use also added to the sacred aura of the place. At that time, all artifacts could be approached by visitors, with no glass barriers blocking the direct connect. A straight link with Sai Baba and his world! Over the years, they have been a witness to changes taking place each time they visit. Baba's articles of daily use have been placed in, glass case which seems to have created a sense of them being exhibits in a museum.

As time passed, and incidents indicative of Baba's presence in their lives increased. She felt a strengthening of faith in this simple, austere Guru. He had summoned us to his Dwarkamai; taken them under his wings.

They were fortunate to have been called by Baba on the day when the palki (palanquin) procession takes place. Though it was a first- time learning, they were blessed and felt immense gratitude by this overwhelming experience. A day of epiphany for them specially Bindu as she could re-discover her spiritual roots, feel a sense of calm prevail and most importantly find her guide and Guru for life. A day of revelations, a perfect miracle all in a day's time! Her non- existent faith changed, the seed of belief and faith had been sown. And as the sapling grew, its roots went deeper with time. She shares gratefully, that in the two decades dedicated to the worship of Sai, she has never for a moment felt lonely, abandoned or distressed. Why? She has placed her hand in His. He leads her family and her, so where is the question of fear?

The holy words of Sri Sai, 'I save my own children, otherwise who else will?'

Jai Sai Ram

From the one learning at Sai's holy feet.

Bindu Midha

Ahmedabad
Mob : (+91) 7410975801
Email : midhabindu@yahoo.co.in

6

BE CAREFUL - ROOPA

It is to be noted here that doubts and difficulties surround us, just to move us and confirm our faith. We are tested as it were. If we hold on steadily to Baba, with full faith and continue our endeavors, our efforts will be ultimately crowned with success. Chapter – XXIX – Shri Sai Satcharita

'Finally done' exclaimed Roopa as she tucked in the last packet of the homemade snack her mom handed to her. She had multiple reasons to be excited to be going on this trip. This would be her very first trip-flight trip, needless to say, her very first international trip too!

'Be very careful Roopa. We are very worried for you. Hope you can manage everything well and land hassle free in Boston' said Roopa's mother. She was naturally worried for Roopa because, they hailed from an interior place called Kavali in Nellore district of Andhra Pradesh.

'Don't worry Amma, all will be well. Dada will be at the airport to receive me once I land in Boston. I am super excited to meet Krishna' Roopa could barely contain her excitement. Roopa's brother lived in Boston and was blessed with a baby girl, Krishna, six months ago. Upon his insistence, Roopa had agreed to visit him in the USA.

The first journey in a flight, that too an international one, coupled with the excitement of meeting up with her brother's family had Roopa jumping in excitement. The chance to meet her new born niece was an icing on the cake.

'Bon voyage Roopa, take care. Do not forget to call us the moment you meet your Dada.' said Roopa's father as he bid his final good bye to her in the Hyderabad airport. Roopa nodded in affirmation. Now she was coming to know that she was slowly getting nervous.

Roopa blindly followed a few co passengers and completed the formalities. She took out the chit that had instructions from her brother.

Check in your baggage at the counter, collect your boarding pass and proceed to security' it read. She made sure, what she was doing and the instructions by her brother matched. She took out her boarding pass and looked at the gate number '2B' it read. She followed the boards and settled down on a chair in front of her assigned gate. She took out the chapati rolls lovingly packed by her mom. She could now feel the hunger pangs. She had not eaten properly for the last two days, as she was in a state of complete excitement. Everything she dreamt of, was now unfolding in front of her as a reality.

'Baba, I can't thank you enough' she said, as she slowly took out Baba's picture she had carefully tucked inside her purse. She offered her gratitude to him and slid the photo back into its place.

'Thank you for flying Air India. We will soon be landing in Boston international airport' the announcement of the pilot woke Roopa up. Her excitement knew no bounds. She was barely one hour away from reuniting with her brother. She hurried in the direction of the washroom, with her cosmetic bag in hand. She freshened up in the excitement of meeting her folks who were so far away from the motherland. All set to meet her brother she came and settled back comfortably in her seat.

The flight landed in Boston. Roopa could hear her own heartbeat. 'Oh god' she thought 'Dada will be so excited to receive me. I hope *Bhabhi* will like the dress I bought. I will cuddle Krishna the moment I go and will take complete care of her till I leave' Roopa's thoughts flowed uninterruptedly.

As the flight landed in Boston, she took out the instructions slip once again. 'Upon landing, follow your co passenger's and head to the immigration counter. Your passport will be stamped' the chit read. 'Everyone will have to clear the immigration process. So, blindly follow your co passengers to the counter' her brother's instructions over the call rang in her ears. She fell in one of the many long queues, and waited impatiently for her turn to get her passport stamped. 'I am just a few minutes away from meeting Dada' she gushed.

'Good morning Mam. May I have your passport' said the stern voice of the officer in front of her. With trembling hands, she handed over her passport to the officer. After glancing through the page that had her visa stamped, the officer stared at her face. The already stern face looked sterner. 'This way Mam' he said, as he summoned a colleague and handed Roopa's passport to the colleague.' next ... His voice called out the next passenger, as Roopa stood there clueless. Another officer who walked in, escorted Roopa to another room that was adjoining the immigration counters. The tension was building and

Roopa had no clue what wrong doing she was being interrogated for.

The impatient officer now spoke 'Madam, do you know you have entered the Unites states of America with a wrong visa? I am sorry, but you have to take the next flight back home.' Roopa was unable to believe what she was hearing. She almost felt the ground beneath her disappear.

'Where are you now headed to?' questioned the officer.

'To my brother's place 'Roopa voice could barely be heard.

'Who will fund an emergency situation that may arise during your stay?' the officer interrogated further.

'My brother sir' replied Roopa.

'Can I have his number?' the officer collected the number and briskly walked away.

Roopa's eyes followed the officer and she could make out that he was talking to her brother over the phone. He disconnected the call, walked in another direction and Roopa could no longer see him. He still held Roopa's passport in hand. Roopa slowly opened her purse and took out Baba's picture. 'Baba, please don't shatter my dreams. I have come all the way to see my brother's family and to see my little Krishna.' she had tears rolling down her eyes. 'Baba, please take me to my brother's house today. I will fast for you on all Thursday's till I am in America'

Almost instantly, the immigration officer walked in. 'We are allowing you to enter our country this time. But, make sure you have a properly stamped visa next time' he said still having the stern look on his face. Roopa could not believe her own ears. She thanked the officer profusely. She gathered herself and walked out of the airport, to be hugged warmly by her brother.

'Dada' she sobbed ...

'Welcome home Roopa. All is well that ends well. Krishna is waiting for you at home. Let's go' he said.

The brother and sister walked towards the car parking. An Indian couple walk past them and she saw a sticker of Baba on the lady's handbag. Baba had given her HIS darshan even in a faraway land.

Feeling doubly reassured, Roopa walked towards the car happily.

Om Sai Ram

Anonymous Devotee

7

SAI GHAR

Blessed are the people of Shirdi, in front of whose houses, Baba stood as a beggar and called out, 'Oh Lassie, give Me a piece of bread' and spread out His hand to receive the same. In one hand He carried a Tumrel (tinpot) and in the other a zoli or choupadari, i.e., a rectangular piece of cloth. Chapter VIII Shri Sai Satcharita

Bikshan Dehi The sadhu called out begging for alms. It was a Thursday and Kavitha had just finished doing aarti to Baba. She came out with some fruits upon hearing the voice. She stood still as she sighted the sadhu. He was clad in a white kafni and a head gear just like Sai Baba. As her eyes fell on the bag that he carried, she was shocked further. The bag resembled the bag that Baba carried too!

She stepped ahead and offered the two bananas and a few oranges she had brought out for him. 'God bless you beti.' said the sadhu. 'You will be very soon going to a place near His abode' he said and walked away.

Kavitha stood a little distraught. The sadhu's words left her a little disturbed. 'What did the sadhu just say' she wondered 'he said I will be soon going near Baba. Does that mean I will be dying an untimely death?' she wondered. 'What will happen to my kids?' tears welled up in her eyes. 'The sadhu may offer some solution to this problem, she thought. She rushed out to see him, but the sadhu was barely in sight, even though it had been just a few minutes.

'Kavitha' her husband's voice interrupted her thoughts. 'Be ready at 5 pm in the evening. The agent has arranged a house for us to buy. We can go and have a look this evening, and if you like it, I shall take the deal forward' he sounded very enthusiastic.

The sadhu's words were still resonating in Kavita's ears. 'Wonder how long I will live in my new house.' Kavitha's husband applied breaks, as he slowed down the car. The couple had set out in the evening to have a look at the property, they intended to buy. 'This is some procession' said her husband as he saw the group approach them. It was more than

50 people who were walking and praising the Leela's of God. They walked in the most disciplined manner. Kavitha and her husband watched as the procession approached them. 'The house is the second on the left there Kavitha, barely 50 metres from here' he said as he waited patiently.

Kavitha could not believe her eyes as the procession approached them. The elaborately dressed Baba's idol and picture sat with all calmness inside the palki. It was Shri Sai Baba's procession that had stopped them before they went to see their dream house. 'This is such a good omen Kavitha' said her husband 'We will now have a look inside and finalize the property'. They saw the Shirdi Sai mandir barely a furlong away from where they stood. Kavitha was overwhelmed and filled with emotions. This is our abode, Vijay. I really don't care how it looks. This is Baba's chosen place for us. Please go ahead and seal the deal.'

'Now I realize what the sadhu Baba said and what weird thoughts I got.' she smiled at herself, as she walked towards Baba's mandir to offer her gratitude. 'Baba, I am near you now, very near' she said as she bowed her head down in gratitude.

Om Sai Ram

Anonymous Devotee

8

KRIPA ON ROOPA

In this connection the following extract from Damu Anna's statement mentioned 'Once when I sat at His Feet along with many others, I had two questions in my mind and He gave answers to both.

(1) There are so many crowding to Sai Baba. Do they all get benefit from Him? To this, He replied orally - 'Look at the mango tree in blossom. If all the flowers brought fruit, what a splendid crop it would be. But do they? Most fall off (either as flowers or as unripe fruits) by wind etc. Very few remain'.

(2) The second question was about myself. If Baba were to pass away, how hopelessly

adrift I would be and how am I to fare then? To this Baba answered that He would be with me when and wherever I thought of Him. That promise He had kept up before 1918 and has been keeping up after 1918. He is still with me. He is still guiding me. This was about 1910-11, when brothers separated from me and my sister died, and there was a theft and police enquiry, all of which incidents upset me very much.
Chapter XXV – Shri Sai Satcharita

The telephone slid from Roopa's hand, as she collapsed on the sofa. She could not believe what her younger brother Arun had just told her over the call. 'Oh God! Let this news turn out to be false' Roopa prayed, as she broke into loud sobs.

Her husband Anand and daughter Amisha, rushed into the living room, as the house resonated with Roopa's sobs. Both were clueless as to why Roopa was sobbing uncontrollably, all of a sudden. Amisha's attention turned to her mom's phone that now lied on the ground, and she realised that it would obviously be a phone call that had shattered Roopa. She signaled the same to her dad. Anand took Roopa's phone and checked who had called Roopa the last. It was Arup, her youngest brother.

Both the dad and his daughter tried to console Roopa and tried to find the reason for the breakdown. All that Roopa was muttering was 'Srikanth' Anand tried calling Srikanth, Roopa's younger brother. The call would not go through. He then called her youngest brother Arup. Arup received his brother in law's call, but he could not utter a single word either. He was crying too. By now Anand realised one thing for sure. The family was staring at some really bad news.

Anand tried to regain his composure, while Amisha forcibly tried to feed her inconsolable mom some water. Anand told his wailing brother-in-law 'Will someone tell me what happened. Arup, compose yourself and tell me what has happened. Are dad and mom, okay?'

Anand was concerned about Roopa's elderly parents, which was quite natural. He sincerely prayed and wished they were okay.

'It's not dad or mom Anand, it's Srikanth. He met with an accident 30 minutes back. I got a call from some onlooker who rushed him to hospital. The hospital has just declared that he was brought in dead.' Arup barely managed to speak. It was now

Anand's turn to freeze. Srikanth was all of 28 years and a dad of 9 months old baby girl.

Roopa hailed from an Iyengar family of Mysore. Her father held the pride of starting one of the first Iyengar bakeries of Mysore. She was the only doting sister of the three brothers. One elder and the other two younger to her. She was now hearing the most devastating news of the death of her younger brother, that too in the most unexpected circumstances.

The next few days zipped past in profound grief, as Roopa struggled to hold the family together, amidst her own sorrow. She had no option, but to be strong for the sake of her aged parents who were battling the grief of the death of their son.

Putra Shokam Nirantaram (the sorrow of the death of a son is continuous), it is said, thought Roopa, as she sat all alone staring into oblivion. Srikanth's smiling face refused to wane from her sight. 'Appa and Amma's grief are multifold more than mine.' Roopa thought 'No parent should ever be cursed to witness the death of their child.' Her thought these days circled only around her late brother and her aged parents.

'Ma' Amisha gently nudged her mother's shoulders as Roopa came out of her thoughts. She looked at Amisha and she felt a chill down her spine as she saw her mother's hollow, dark circled eyes. 'What are you doing to yourself Amma' Amisha pleaded. 'Mama (uncle) will never come back however much you cry. You came and sit in this balcony, as I was leaving to college at 10 am. It is now almost 4 pm and you haven't eaten a morsel, Amma' Amisha pleaded. Amisha had seen her mom turn into an emotional wreck in the last few days. The happy smiling face of Roopa, now seemed a thing of the past.

'Smitha, I have never seen Amma so distressed ever in her life. She neither eats nor drinks properly after Mama's death.' Amisha was in tears as she confided in her best friend. Both were college going girls, and handling this kind of a situation, was beyond their maturity limits. Wanting to see her best friend and her favorite aunty happy, Smitha just did what she could think of at that moment. 'Take Baba home Amisha and you pray to him. see what wonders can happen', she spoke as she handed a small statue and a picture of Sai Baba.

Till then, Amisha never knew about Baba. The moment she held Baba in her hand, she felt a strange energy flow in her. She now was confident that her mom will slowly start to recover. She gently held Sai in her hand, caressed him carefully, and took him near her heart saying 'Baba you are my only hope.'

She headed home with a sprint in her steps. She already imagined her mom's smiling beautiful face. With these positive thoughts, she rang the doorbell 'Amma, see who came home.' Roopa, stared at the child like Sai in her child's arm. She for a moment felt, she saw her Srikanth's smiling face in Baba's face'. Amisha, stand where you are. Do not enter, exclaimed Roopa, as she hurriedly went in. Amisha stood there, a little worried, as she did not understand what made her mom make her wait outside.

Roopa came from her pooja room with an aarthi in her hand. With pure bliss, love and happiness, she performed aarthi to Sai and spoke

WELCOME HOME SAI

'You have brought Sai to our house without even any prior discussion Amisha, he has chosen to come to our house, amongst the lakhs of other houses in Mysore. Are we not blessed?' said Roopa.

The mother and daughter, carefully placed him in their pooja room.

Little did Roopa realise, A new chapter in her life would unfold with the blessings of Sai. Sai made his way into Roopa's house and her heart. From that day, Roopa became an ardent devotee of Baba and regularly read Sai Satcharita.

Slowly, she witnessed her life change for better in all ways, professionally and personally.

Fast Forward 10 Years.

'Can we have a word, Roopa?' said Anand as he held the phone in his hand 'It's a bit urgent'

'2 minutes,' signaled Roopa as she finished doing Saivaar aarthi to her Baba.

'The groom's father has called back' said Anand 'They seem to be interested in taking forward our daughter's proposal. I also think there is no reason for us to negate the proposal, Roopa. The boy is a Dentist, they are a very educated and cultured family, so there is nothing that should stop us. This is the best we can expect for our daughter Amisha' the fatherly concern was quite evident.

'Baba, you know what is best for my child. She is not my child, but she is Yours' said Roopa, as she smiled at Anand, with a signal to go ahead. She felt a strange peace, as she mentally prepared to conduct the wedding of her only daughter Amisha, with Baba's guidance. 'All HIS WISH' thought Roopa.

Days passed...

The sound of the door-bell once again brought Roopa back into reality. She got up from her sofa and opened the main door, to the smiling faces of Amisha and Shreyas. 'Mom, take the prasad. We had gone to Baba's mandir ahead of our first wedding anniversary' both of them touched her feet to seek blessings.

'Baba bless you my children,' said Roopa.

Happiness filled to the brim. Roopa looked at Baba's murthi in her pooja room. No words needed to be spoken between the Guru and his devotee!

Om Sai Ram

Anonymous Devotee

9

A LIFE SAVED

The merciful Baba comforted them saying 'Those who resort to this Masjid shall never suffer anything in this life and to the end of time. Be now worry! Apply Udi on the abcess and within a week he will recover. Believe in God! This is no Masjid, but Dwarkamai. He who steps here, will soon get health and happiness and his sufferings will come to an end'. Chapter XXXIV- Shri Sai Satcharita

Following story has been narrated by a staunch and a very vetron devotee of Sai, Mr. V Sundaram who is 83 years now. He is connected with Sai since 1980. A few articles by him have been printed in Sai Leela Magazine in the years 1981-83.

Mr. Sundaram narrates...

The following incident occurred long time ago in the mid-fifties (1954-55) in the family of late P.S. Varadaraja Iyer. Ramaiya mama (uncle) was my (V. Sundaram) mother's own younger brother who had a wife named Thangam. Thangam means gold in Tamil and no doubt my auntie really had a golden heart.

My uncle Ramaiya mama and auntie Thangam used to visit us from Behala to our house in Rashbehari Avenue Calcutta. Though my auntie was very kind and helpful yet she had a very bad Fitz problem. She was a Fits patient. During my school years, I remember whenever she used to visit us with my uncle, me and my other brothers used to sit near our auntie to listen to her interesting stories. But our parents used to warn us not to sit close to her as she was a Fits patient else, we may get hurt if she gets Fits suddenly. Whenever she used to get Fits, she used to shout like a devil and fall getting hurt herself and others who were sitting near her. As we were all school going children that time, we used to get shocked to hear when she used to scream and fall. It so happened one day during their visit to our house, on the second-floor veranda she waved her hand to her beloved husband down the lane who was just going to office. Just then she was attacked by this horrible Fits. Poor Ramaiya's wife fell down screaming from the second-floor veranda down the lane. Uncle Ramaiya mama lifted her and brought her home to the second floor.

Ordinarily anyone in that state would have collapsed falling from the second-floor veranda to the ground on the lane. Believe it or not to the surprise of everyone around friends, relatives, neighbours and others she had minor fracture that needed slight medication coupled with Shirdi Sai Baba's miracle 'UDI' (the grey ash powder)! In due course my auntie became alright and began to carry on her usual household routine life. Much later the couple that is my uncle Ramaiya mama and his wife Thangam were blessed with a very fair robust chubby looking cute little boy who the family members gave the name of Sai Ram. He grew up to become a young talented singer. Again, after the demise of his mother he was blessed to get a mother-in-law bearing the same name as Thangam a robust young lady who took great care of Sai Ram and looked after him more than her own son. Sri Sai Baba's Miracle is unfathomable. Finally, my own youngest brother also bears the name of Sai Ram retired from HSCL as Finance Manager.

In conclusion each one of the Sai devotees might have experienced extraordinary levels of higher consciousness in their own life or many others may be wanting to share their feelings, thoughts and views with Sri. Sujay Khandelwal in the years to come.

Om Sai Ram
In Sai service

V Sundaram

Kolkata
Mob : (+91) 6289454595
Email : vsundaramiyer@gmail.com

10

SHIRDI'S SOIL HEALS

However, oppressed and troubled one may be as soon as he steps into the Masjid, he is on the pathway to happiness. The Fakir here is very kind and He will cure the disease, and protect all with love and kindness.' Chapter XIII – Shri Sai Satcharita

Anandi pulled the thermometer out of her son's armpit. The lines of worry again appeared on her forehead as it read 101°C. 'Put wet cloth on his forehead and see the doctor tomorrow morning' said her husband, Rajesh. Both of them were very worried about their 5 year old son who was running fever for the last 5 days.

Anandi and Rajesh had with great difficulty managed to get the tickets to Manmad. Their long impending Shirdi trip was due to happen after months of planning, as Rajesh had used up all his contacts to manage two tickets to Manmad in the overcrowded train that ran on that route. When the plan was about to materialise, Akhil, their 5-year-old son fell sick severely dampening their spirits.

The child was getting fever every six hours, and Anandi braced herself to spend another sleepless night. Akhil was not even able to take in a drop of water, let alone any food. Everything Anandi tried to forcibly feed him; he was throwing up.

'Does it pain here?' asked the doctor as she gently pressed his stomach, the next morning.

'No' said the child in a feeble voice. 5 days of fever had left the child very weak.

'Here?' the doctor's hand gently moved to the other side.

'No doctor' answered the child.

She stood in front of the child silently for a moment, trying to figure out what was wrong. She was no ordinary doctor, 3 decades of experience as a physician was behind her. Being a staunch devotee of Baba herself, Doctor clearly knew he was testing her patience. The doctor came and settled on her chair, as the child walked from the examination table to sit beside his mother. Anandi was a worried mom now, she was also very concerned about their impending Shirdi trip, which was being now materialised after years of planning.

'Anandi' said the doctor as she leaned on her chair 'Continue with your trip. I see that there is no infection in Akhil. My experience says that it is a bout of some virus. He will fight it out and of course, Baba will help him to fight it out.' She was looking at the Baba idol she had placed on her table as she spoke. 'Here, I have written the medicines to stop vomiting and fever.' said the doctor as she handed the prescription. 'Go ahead with your trip by placing your entire trust on Baba, believe me, he will be fine.' 'Thank you doctor' said Anandi, as she walked out of her clinic with a lot of apprehensions in her mind.

Akhil was still running fever as they boarded their train the next day. Vomiting had not stopped either. Anandi kept praying to Baba as she boarded the train.

Room number 220, said the receptionist as she handed the keys to Rajesh. The couple had finally landed in Shirdi with their sick child and checked into a hotel called 'Bayijaa Maa'. 'We are now in safe hands' Rajesh thought. The couple walked briskly towards the room with their sick child in hand. 'Do not worry Anandi. We are here for three days and we will surely get Baba's darshan. Akhil will be alright' Rajesh tried to console his distraught wife.

They settled in their room and tried to get some sleep. They had done an overnight journey in a train with a sick child which had let the couple drained mentally and physically. Their heavy eyelids closed and all three slid into deep sleep almost instantly.

'Mummy…Mummy' the child's nudging and calling woke Anandi up.

'Yes beta' she said anticipating that he will ask her to escort him to wash room to throw up.

'I am very hungry. Can I have something to eat please' asked the child, and Anandi could not believe her own ears.

She instantly took the intercom and dialed the reception ordering for some khichdi. It had been almost 5 days since her child had eaten. Akhil ate the khichdi, as if he had not eaten forever. The next 2 hours was spent anxiously by the parents. They were not very sure if the sick child would actually digest the food. Much to their relief, the next two hours were uneventful. Anandi peeped out of her hotel window to see the mandir gopuram and caught a glimpse of the orange flag that was swaying gracefully to the wind. 'Baba teri leela apaar (Sai your miracles have no boundaries). We have passed all the tests you put us through and we are here to see you.' she smiled.

'Sai rehem nazar karna, bacchon ka paalan karna' the couple sang, as they held their child lovingly. Their unstinted belief in Baba was proven yet again.

Anonymous Devotee

11

QUEUE RESCHEDULLED

There lived in Bandra (a suburb of Bombay) a Tendulkar family, all the members of which were devoted to Baba. Mrs. Savitribai Tendulkar has published a Marathi book named 'Shri Sainath Bhajan Mala' containing 800 abhangas and padas describing the Leelas of Baba. It is a book worth reading by those who are interested in Baba. The son, Babu Tendulkar was studying hard day and night and wanted to appear for the medical examination. He consulted some astrologers. Examining his horoscope they told him that the stars were not favourable that year and that he should appear for the examination next year, when he would be certainly successful. This cast a gloom over him and made him restless. A few days afterwards his mother went to Shirdi and saw Baba. Amongst other things she mentioned the gloomy and morose condition of her son, who was to appear for the examination in a few days. Hearing this Baba said to her, 'Tell your son to believe in Me, to throw aside horoscopes and predictions of astrologers and palmists and go on with his studies. Let him appear for the examination with a calm mind, he is sure to pass this year. Ask him to trust in Me and not to get disappointed'. The mother returned home and communicated Baba's message to her son. Then he studied hard and in due course appeared for the examination. In the written papers he did well, but being overwhelmed by doubts he thought that he would not secure sufficient marks for passing. So he did not care to appear for the oral examination. But the examiner was after him. He sent word through a fellow- student, stating that he had passed in the written examination and that he should appear for the oral. The son being thus encouraged appeared for the oral examination and was successful in both. Thus he got through the examination that year successfully by Baba's grace, though the stars were against him. It is to be noted here that doubts and difficulties surround us just to move us and confirm our faith. We are tested as it were. If we hold on steadily to Baba, with full faith and continue our endeavours, our efforts will be ultimately crowned with success. Chapter XXIX - Shri Sai Satcharita

Till 2009 Banani Bose didn't know much about Sai Baba, only knew the fact that there was a saint by the name of Sai Baba who lived in Shirdi during his lifetime. And today she is an ardent devotee who experiences miracles of Baba, day in and day out. Out of the numerous miracles she narrates the following....

In the year 2009 she shifted house. The building she moved into has 50 flats and community hall where all meetings and events used to take place. One day all the residents met at the building community Hall to get acquainted to each other for good. There Banani met a lady by the name of Ruchi Seth along with many others like her. It was a casual meeting which ended and all residents were back to their respective flats. After almost 3 months the same lady Ruchi Seth came to Banani's flat and gifted her a photo of Sai Baba which she had got from Shirdi. Banani was pleasantly surprised and perplexed also that how can anyone after just one meeting, that too three months back suddenly come to her home and gifted her a picture of Lord Sai.

Banani being a spiritual person, involved into regular Pooja and prayers at her house, was very happy that she received the picture of Sai and thanked Ruchi immensely for the same. Ruchi then told her that she also was quite surprised that she brought this picture for Banani as they hardly knew each other and had met only once, still she remembered her during her Shirdi visit and was almost compelled to buy the picture for Banani as if somebody had instructed her to do so. Banani was pleasantly surprised and happy at this happening as she was sure that Baba himself wanted to come to her house. She knew that Sai Baba was such a guru who used to choose his disciples himself and then bless them accordingly. This was how Sai Baba came to Banani's home for the first time and it was the first miracle of Baba in her life.

In 2012 Banani's son had his board examination of 12th standard and he was quite nervous as he didn't cover the entire syllabus and was afraid that if he were tested on portions that he didn't prepare he would not pass. Likewise, Banani also became nervous and was telling her son that what can be done at this last hour. Meantime Banani's friend came to their house and gave them Prasad, Sacred thread and photo of Sai Baba which she brought for them from Shirdi itself. After handing over the Prasad, she left and Banani told his son to have Prasad and leave rest to Baba. She also said to her son that pray to Baba that everything goes well. Son reached school and since it was Practical projects exam, they were allotted project numbers. To the horror and dismay of his Son he was assigned a project which he didn't prepare. But having no other options he stood in queue and waited for his turn. There were two queues of Students who were moving number-wise. He silently prayed to Baba and stood there. Just as his number was about to come the examiner called it a Tiffin break and would resume after the break.

After the break a new examiner came and he instructed to merge both the queues of students as he felt it was unnecessary for separate queues. This merging of Queues was no less than a miracle as Banani's son new assignment was known to him which happened only because this shuffle took place. He could not believe his good luck and thanked Baba for taking him out of this grave situation so smoothly. His faith towards Baba now grew. And on his result day miracles showered on them as when he opened the laptop first thing that came on screen was Baba's picture in a blessing pose and surely, he was blessed with success. He secured very good marks more than he and parents expected.

This incident and others instilled deep faith in Banani towards Baba and she started performing daily Pooja with utmost devotion. She always prayed to Baba to grant her Shraddha and Saburi. She started conversing with Baba and prayed always to grant her patience as she thought she became very restless at times and lost control of her emotions. Like every one she also landed in problems often but Baba always guided her out of it soon.

Once she performed a five-day Sai Vrat and did it very meticulously. On the last day of Vrat in the morning she saw a picture of Baba which carried a message which was as follows:

Read Sai Satcharita

Chant my 108 names

I will come to you anyway

Reading this she thought, first two mentioned were okay, as she was already doing Vrat in which she was doing both mentioned advice but was wondering how will the third mentioned line come true...

'I will come to you anyway'. Nonetheless the day rolled on and was exceptionally busy as her students had music exams that day as she is a music teacher.

On Vrat day she was supposed to give Prasad to 5 ladies as a ritual. Being a very busy day, she couldn't go out to distribute Prasad instead gave Prasad to four ladies (mothers of her students) who had come along with their kids. Now at the end of day she was to give Prasad to one more lady and was wondering what to do. It was almost 10pm in the night and she had to complete the rituals of her Vrat. Suddenly she remembered she can give Prasad to fifth lady named Ashu who was herself a Sai devotee and used to live nearby in another apartment. She immediately called up Ashu and expressed her wish to give Prasad to Ashu and she readily agreed. But since it was late in night Banani didn't want to go up to her flat and requested her to come down to collect the Prasad. When Banani and her husband reached Ashu's building they called her to come down to collect the Prasad. Ashu refused to come down but instead requested Banani to come over to her flat. Initially Banani was reluctant but ultimately gave in to request of Ashu and went up to her flat. When the door of her flat opened she was standing with a photo of Sai Baba. Ashu then revealed that she had brought this picture of Baba for Banani from Shirdi and wanted to give her that day itself and that's why forced Banani to come up. Banani was surprised and overwhelmed and realised that what she read in Morning... 'I will come to you anyway' came true...

This miracle of Baba was such a pleasant episode in Banani's life which she can never forget in her lifetime and reminded her of Baba's words.

'Whatever I say always comes true'

Banani Bose

Kuwait
Mob : (+) 96566385943
Email : b.bose29@gmail.com

12

SAI BRINGS BACK HOPE

Mr. Gopal Narayan Ambadekar of Poona was a devotee of Baba. He served for ten years in the Abkari department in the Thana District and in Javhar state, from where he had to retire. He tried to get some other job, but he did not succeed. He was overtaken by other calamities and his condition grew from bad to worse. He passed 7 years in this condition, visiting Shirdi every year and placing his grievance before Baba. In 1916 his plight became worst and be decided to commit suicide in Shirdi. So he came there with his wife and stayed for two months. One night while sitting in a bullock cart in front of Dixit's Wada, he resolved to end his life by throwing himself into a well close by. He proposed to do one way but Baba wished to do something else. A few paces from this place, there was a hotel and its proprietor Mr. Sagun, a devotee of Baba, came out and accosted him thus - 'Did you ever read this Akkalkotkar Maharaja's life?' Ambadekar took that book from Sagun and began to read it. Casually, or we may say providentially he came across a story which was to this effect. During the life time of Akkalkotkar Maharaj a certain devotee suffered very much from an incurble disease and when he could endure the agony and pain no longer, he became desperate and to end his miseries threw himself one night into a well. Immediately the Maharaj came there and took him out with his own hands and advised him thus - 'You must enjoy the fruit - good or bad - of your past actions; if the enjoyment be incomplete, suicide won't help you. You have to take another birth and suffer again; so instead of killing yourself, why not suffer for some time and finish up your store of the fruit of your past deeds and be done with it once and for all?' Chapter XXVI - Shri Sai Satcharita

Bindi Bindi… a voice came which only she could hear. Bindi woke up in utter tiredness, trying to find out who called her. Must be someone close as this was the nick name of Bindhya Subba who is from the hills of Kurseong, Darjeeling. Her sleep vanished as she realized it was a call from inside.

It was late afternoon time and she was trying to sleep as she was extremely tired after a super hectic day that Thursday managing house hold chores. Bindi is an evolving Sai devotee who has joined a Mahaparayan group to read 2 chapters of Sai Satcharita every Thursday for the last 2 years. That day being a Thursday, she was supposed to read the chapters but due to tiredness she thought of choosing sleep by skipping reading and telling Baba 'Baba, Baba… I'm so tired and sleepy today, I won't be doing Parayan'. But Sai had a different wish. The moment she got sleep, HE woke her up calling her from inside, Bindi Bindi, which she realized after introspecting her soul. She realised Sai himself woke her up and that Sai wants her to read and thus he woke her up from sleep. She started reading immediately and instead of 2 she read 3 chapters by mistake.

Bindi got connected to Sai in 2020 when she was going through a depression and had suicidal thoughts. She didn't know what to do. Life had become so meaningless for her that she thought of killing herself. One day suddenly she got a thought to worship Saibaba. Her sister had a picture in which Sai Baba was there and Sai himself inspired her to get connected to Him. She started surfing social media and google to know more about Him where she came across a Mahaparayan group and joined it instantly and since then she is in unconditional bhakti of Sai.

Once so happened that she woke up on a Thursday with an acute pain in her stomach. She realised the pain was because of constipation which was so acute that she couldn't move out of bed. Question of reading 2 chapters arose in her mind but her body and mind didn't support. She prayed to Sai....

Baba mujhe theek karoo mujhe Parayan karna hain. Mujhe khud karna hain, volunteer nahi chahiya

Baba, please cure me as I want to do my Parayan. I want to do myself without anyone to volunteer for me.

Baba listened to her prayer and showered her blessings in such a way that within sometime all her pain vanished and she bathed and did her Parayan as usual and since then she didn't get any discomfort on any Thursday and is continuing with Parayan, religiously with full faith and devotion.

Now Bindi wants to do Parayan for her lifetime to know more and more about her Sai. She does pooja daily and special ones on Thursday. Her faith in Baba is increasing each passing day and from where she used to feel her life to be a burden its slowly blossoming like a flower.

Sai has his own ways to bring about hope from the state of hopelessness which is depicted from the life of Bindi.

Bindhya Subba
Darjeeling
Email : subbabindhya76@gmail.com

SAI THE SAVIOUR

'One must enjoy the fruit - good or bad - of your past actions; if the enjoyment be incomplete, suicide won't help you. You have to take another birth and suffer again; so instead of killing yourself, why not suffer for some time and finish up your store of the fruit of your past deeds and be done with it once and for all?' Chapter XXVI – Shri Sai Satcharita

Till 2017 Deep was quite unaware of Sai Baba and knew Him only through his friend who used to visit Shirdi with his wife. He made an ad hoc request to his friend to get a picture of Sai from Shirdi very casually without much expectations or plan. To his surprise his friend got him a beautiful picture of Baba which then Deep adorned in his house. This was how Sai Baba manifested himself in Deep's house without any paraphernalia. And today Deep feels every breath he takes is a blessing of lord Sai and Sai is only way to happiness and peace. He feels HIS mercy and grace, each moment of his life.

Couple of years passed and in 2019, Deep suddenly fell ill with a severe neurological disorder, known case of Chronic neuropathy which rendered him in state which can be called a special situation where he almost lost his mobility. Friends and family were by his side but loss of job played the silent killer's role and he went into a state of depression.

In 2020 the menace of COVID hit the entire world and India was also under prolonged lockdown which disturbed the entire logistics of medical world and new protocol were in place to even get hospitalized for treatment. In such scenario around 1st week of May Deep fell seriously ill which needed immediate hospitalisation and after being in isolation room for 48 hours his actual treatment started and was shifted to a single room where he could meet his family once a day. His infection was addressed and was getting better but on 4th day morning he started vomiting profusely which disturbed other essential parameters of body. In about 3 hours from then he started feeling he was losing his voice and his jawline was getting twisted and fist/palms refused to open. Doctor gave him an emergency injection and sent him for MRI scan and then to be immediately shifted to ICU.

He was thinking he had stroke of paralysis and after losing mobility of lower limbs, he was going to lose his hands too. On way to MRI scan on a stretcher though he was feeling drowsy, but continued praying to Sai to save him and not make him completely handicapped. He felt asleep and, in his trance, he felt he was falling in deep dark tunnel very rapidly and there was no end to the tunnel. He got scared and thought his end had come... There appeared a bright light and his rapid fall was arrested and as he thought he had reached the end of tunnel, suddenly he saw Sai Baba in his ever-magnanimous form in his blessings posture the same he had in his house. His falling feeling stopped, darkness disappeared and emerged Sri Saibaba with a Helios. He didn't remember anything after that...

After 6 hours of deep slumber, he woke up to find himself in ICU surrounded by Medical equipment's and nurses. He recalled what had happened to him a few hours back and tried to talk and could hear his voice. He tried opening his fists and slowly by grace of Sai he was able to stretch and move his hands which were frozen a few hours back. A new lease of life for Deep by grace of Sai.

Since that day Sai is the way of life for him. He lives and breathes Sai, Sai, Sai and Sai also never ceases to amase him with miracles almost every day in his life.

Sainath Maharaj ki Jai

Deep Khemka

Kolkata
Mob : (+91) 9830980833
Email : 2deepkhemka@gmail.com

14

CLOSE DOORS OPENED

His practice was to worship all the Gods in the village, and then come to the Masjid, and after saluting Baba's gadi (asan) he worshipped Baba, and after doing some service (shampooing His Legs) drank the washings (Tirth) of Baba's Feet. Once it so happened that he came to the Masjid, without worshipping God Khandoba, as the door of the temple was closed. Baba did not accept his worship, and sent him again, saying that the door was open then. Megha went, found the door open, worshipped the Deity and then returned to Baba as usual. Chapter XXVIII – Shri Sai Satcharita

Sairam Uncle hurriedly walked out of the compound of his house and called out for his driver Hemanth.

'I see that you turned up late today. Don't you know it's a Thursday and a Saivaar? Don't you know that I need to go to the mandir? Are you taking advantage of the fact that I am not able to drive and I depend on you?' Sairam uncle a retired senior citizen was in the evening of his life and lived away from his children in his own house all by himself. He was dependent on his driver Hemanth to run even the smallest of errands, as he suffered from a week knee which had left him immobile for sometime. He walks visibly upset with his driver, with each passing minute, his eagerness to see his Guru only increased.

Hemanth realised his mistake and apologized to his Sir. The car zoomed in the direction of Sai mandir.

Meanwhile in the mandir, The Pandit Arun Sai prepared to close the door for the day and allow Baba to rest. 'The day was so blissful Baba.' he mused as he pulled the mosquito curtains on Baba. 'But I wonder why Sairam uncle did not turn up today' He delayed closing the main door of the mandir by another 10 minutes. He started some basic cleaning, so that he could stay there for that extra 10 minutes. 'I hope uncle is well, he said to himself. He is old and his children live abroad, there is no chance of him coming in so late'. Arun Sai made up his mind and locked the temple door.

His mind was completely preoccupied with uncle's thoughts. There was not a single week uncle missed the darshan of Baba on a Thursday, so long as Arun Sai remembered. Whenever he visited his children or had some pre occupation, uncle would always inform Arun about his absence that particular week. Lost in uncle's thoughts, Arun bowed down to Baba before he bid him a good night. He pulled the huge carved wooden door, locked it and walked towards his two-wheeler. He was just about to start his bike when he again got a doubt whether he had locked the door properly. He came back walking towards the mandir, rechecked the door, wished the security guard a good night and left for the day.

15-20 minutes after Arun Sai left, Sairam uncle reached the temple. Seeing the temple locked, tears welled up in his eyes. 'Saab, pandit ji just left closing the mandir. Today you are late. You may want to come tomorrow morning for the darshan' the security guard informed. Sairam uncle, just walked with a sad expression on his face and sat on a bench in the premises of the mandir, disheartened.

'Baba you know I am old and dependent. In spite of that you decided not to give me darshan today' uncle sobbed. He sat there chanting his favorite Sai Gayathri Mantra. 'You are omnipresent so I will sit here in your premises and go home. I will come again for your darshan coming week.' He sat in the peaceful premises of the temple and prayed.

'Sir, its past your regular dinner time. You need to take your medicines Sir. Can we leave now?' Hemanth's voice brought uncle back into the world. He nodded his head in acceptance. Imagining the holy feet of Baba, he walked to the mandir entrance and bowed his head down in front of the main door. To his utter surprise, the huge wooden door moved slightly. He was taken aback and gently pushed the door with his hands. The door completely opened, as Sairam uncle, Hemanth and the security guard stood in complete bewilderment. Baba was there, giving his darshan in his complete glory to his bhakt (devotee).

The pandit Arun Sai was informed and called back. Soon he arrived riding his bike. Upon his arrival, no one spoke a word. The Leela was beyond the eloquence of the pandit or the bhakt.

The temple was locked again and everyone left that night filled with gratitude and immersed in Baba's unbelievable Leela.

Om Sai Ram

Anonymous Devotee

MY NAUGHTY BOY - MY SAI

One day at noon after the Arti, devotees were returning to their lodgings, when Baba gave the following beautiful advice:

'Be wherever you like, do whatever you choose, remember this well that all what you do is known to Me. I am the Inner Ruler of all and seated in their hearts. I envelope all the creatures, the movable and im-movable world. I am the Controller - the wire-puller of the show of this Universe. I am the mother - origin of all beings - the Harmony of three Gunas, the propeller of all senses, the Creator, Preserver and Destroyer. Nothing will harm him, who turns his attention towards Me, but Maya will lash or whip him who forgets Me. All the insects, ants, the visible, movable *and immovable world, is My Body or Form'. Hearing these beautiful and precious words, I at once decided in my mind to serve no man henceforward, but my Guru only. Chapter III - Shri Sai Satcharita*

Only when the devotee is bursting with love and devotion, Vitthal will manifest Himself here. Chapter IV - Shri Sai Satcharita

Shirdi Sai Baba came to her when Sanskriti was 3 years of age. Since then, till now and beyond, she will always be a Sai Baba devotee. Her first visit to Shirdi was in the year 1993-94 at the tender age of 4. Her family would always say, she used to touch the feet of Sai Baba in Dwarkamai many times. At that age, would say, she knew nothing about Shirdi Sai Baba and yet had a devotion which is beyond words of expression. Today, she is a staunch Sai Baba devotee. Any temple she goes, the first line which comes to her is 'Om Sai Ram' and whichever God is in front of her eyes, looks like Sai to her. Sai Baba has done a lot for her. Having faced many challenges in life but Sai has always given her the strength and courage to face it and come out of it successfully.

Her life is incomplete without Sai Baba. Whether happy or sad, she would visit the temple once in a day for Aarthi. She is living because of Him. And it is always nice to be in the presence of Him and His Leelas.

She lovingly calls Sai Baba as naughty boy:)... He is very naughty with her... She often goes on strikes too on Sai Baba and He answers within 3 days of doing strike. He has taught her both Shraddha (Faith) and Saburi (Patience) through every experience and challenge in life. When she prays to him with love and ask Him, he will take her Saburi test but when she says 'I will go on strike or What the hell do you think you are doing, you Naughty Boy?' he comes and answers her prayer. At times Baba is Tom, She is Jerry and they keep running behind each other and inseparable for ever to eternity and beyond. Well, Baba bears all her tantrums and still loves unconditionally.

In any challenging situation automatically, it comes 'Baba please come and help' and He comes and without even her realising He will give a solution. No matter what, Baba has always been there for her and He will always be there for her forever.

Though she has many experiences but she narrates a few of them:

Sai cures barking Cough

Sai Baba loves His devotees and never allows them to suffer. She had a strange cough called as 'barking cough'. A cough which has no medicine and it just goes away only in the temple with meditation on Sai Baba. She has been suffering for many years from this strange cough. Every time she used to get this cough, the only medicine for this is praying to Sai Baba with the Aarthi. Finally, Baba cured her from this which even medicines could not. Great are the ways of Sai Baba to save His devotees from health issues.

Om Sai Ram

Sai cures Epilepsy

She was on sodium valproate for many years for epilepsy. She used to get fits. One fine day during her BBM days Baba came in her dream and said 'Come to Shirdi and put your medicine in the Hundi and you will be fine.' She followed her dream. One fine day she left for Shirdi, put the medicine in the hundi and said to Baba that she was stopping her medicine and requested Baba to take care of her. It's been more than 15 years now and she is out of medication and completely epilepsy free. Baba cured her completely from the health issue. Great is Baba's ways of curing diseases.

Om Sai Ram

Sai's presence during Abhishekam

26 November, 2015 is a significant day for Sanskriti. Every Thursday is significant as it's Sai day. On this day, she did Abhishekam for the first time in a temple near her house. 'Every deed done is a blessing from Sai,' is the way she looked at it. That day she got up at 4 am in the morning, got ready and went to the temple. Anything she does on a Thursday, it's a blessing one as she was fasting and it was a very nice feeling for her to be in the presence of Sai. That day, she was the first person to start the Abhishekam (consecration). Purohit ji gave her some milk in the Shankh (shell). He put little milk only but the quantity of the milk increased more than what was being put by the purohit. The joy of the purohit knew no bounds and he told her to come and do Abhishekam every Thursday. Great are Sai's ways of bringing His devotees to him.

Om Sai Ram

Sai shows His presence during Aarthi

In a Baba temple little on the outskirts of Bangalore where she goes once in a while, in that temple where they allow devotees to do the Aarthi for Baba. It was Madhyan Aarthi and she was doing Aarthi for Baba and the person who built the temple, Nagaraj uncle, had taken a video of her doing Aarthi. In one corner there was a Hanuman ji idol and on top of that on the gopuram Baba is sitting there and watching her do Aarthi. Baba also had come in shadow form in that temple and saw her do Aarthi. Great are Baba's ways of being there for His devotees.

Om Sai Ram

Sai appears in Shirdi in the form of a Purohit

In Shirdi she did not have Aarthi pass and she was roaming as usual between Chavadi and Dwarkamai talking to security uncle and aunty. Aunty-Uncle! Aunty-Uncle! she kept on over there. She sat outside Dwarkamai along with many other devotees. Out of nowhere comes the Purohit, whom she knew, spotted her and asked, 'Why are you sitting here?'. She said 'I do not have pass and I am sitting for Aarthi.' He told her to come with him and took her inside the main mandir bye-passing the queue. She went directly inside and sat right in front of Baba in the center and did afternoon Aarthi in the main mandir. Baba made the purohit give her sweet rice as prasadam and literally fed her. She had rice after 7 years because she had a *mannat* (vow) and had given up rice for it. It was her prayer to have rice in Shirdi and Baba answered by feeding her with rice in main mandir Shirdi. She was literally crying the whole-time during Aarthi. Purohit ji introduced her to some stranger Sai devotee who said 'I am a humble PhD who does a lot of things silently. I am Baba's child who comes to Shirdi every year and gives him *ittar* (perfume) and *vastra* (cloth).' She had ittar and vastra with her thinking where to give them and after hearing this out she instantly gave them to him.

After she came back to the room and had her mobile, she called the purohit to thank him for giving her such a lovely darshan and the purohit said he did not even see her at all. She realised then that It was Baba who came to her in the form of purohit. Baba is great.

Om Sai Ram

Sai appears in the form of an old man

In Shirdi she usually gives vastras everywhere she went. One fine day she had a plan to take vastra to Vitthal ji mandir and she was waiting for an auto. She had her phone because she had a plan of going to Dwarkamai which she thought she would do after she returned from Vitthal ji temple and was waiting for an auto near her hotel. Her naughty boy's plans were different. An old man comes to her and asked 'Why are you waiting here?' She replied that she was going to Vitthal temple. 'No, you come with me' instructed the old man. 'I have my phone with me and I can't go inside Dwarkamai or Samadhi-mandir as they will not allow phone inside' replied Sanskriti. 'Don't worry I will take care of everything. You just come with me.' confirmed the old man. She said okay!

The phone was get detected in the scanner of both Dwarkamai and Samadhi mandir. It is humanly not possible for the phone not to be detected, and no one checked or asked her anything. She was shocked beyond words. 'He took me inside without making me stand in queue. He took me directly to Dwarkamai and near the Dhuni. He made me sit there for 10 minutes where I did my meditation. He waited till I finished my meditation' surprisingly said Sanskriti. Then he took her to the main mandir through a route that she has not seen till date. The magic of Naughty boy continues – the time was around 9.30 am and Chota Aarthi does not happen at that time. He took her inside the main mandir, told the purohit to set the Pancha Aarthi thali and made her do Chota Aarthi in the main temple (this is usually done by men and they don't allow ladies to do it). The purohits did not say anything and just did it. She was inside the main mandir and was sobbing and froze literally. After doing the Aarthi she turned back to say Sairam thank you and the old man wasn't there. She got goosebumps by the way Baba shows Himself to His devotees.

Sai is her best friend and partner in crime and she is always grateful to Him for all His blessings on her.

Om Sai Ram

Sai Sanskriti

Bangalore
Mob : (+91) 9148366659
Email : drsaisanskrithi@gmail.com

16

9 PACKETS OF UDI

Baba said to Megha - 'I require no door to enter. I have no form nor any extension; I always live everywhere. I carry on, as a wirepuller, of all the actions of the man who trusts Me and merges in Me.' Chapter XXVIII – Shri Sai Satcharita

April 2021, Jyoti was twisting in her bed in her house in Gurgaon due to unbearable pain in her stomach. She was undergoing a treatment for some time now but all in vain. She was having sleepless nights and days due to continued pain. During this time, one day she came across some old serial on Sai Baba, which she started watching. It interested her so much that she watched all the 68 episodes of the series. Meanwhile she started googling to know more about Sai. One night at 2 am Jyoti woke up in her sleep while she was dreaming. Sai had come in her dream and asked her to do Sai

Sandhya that day at 7.16 pm. She was not aware then, what Sai Sandhya was all about and how to do it. Half asleep she couldn't stop herself from searching about it and got some idea. Later, in the evening, she opened a link and did it online with the help of YouTube. This was the beginning of Jyoti's connection with Sai and now her life revolves around Sai.

She kept searching about Sai on internet and ordered the holy book, *Shri Sai Satcharita*, from Flipkart and started reading. Her health would not permit her to read much as she couldn't sit up most of the times. It took her nearly 3 months to complete her 1st read of the book then. There after she has read it countless number of times as she read daily. She has participated in many Satcharita Quiz contests and won innumerable prizes in a short span of time. Now Sai Baba is everything to her.

With the blessings of Sai, she started recovering when one fine day in 2022 her husband had an acute stomach pain. In 2015 he had gone through angioplasty and a stent was inserted in his heart and they, all including their son got really worried as to what happened now. Immediately he was taken to a nearby hospital and admitted in Emergency. Since morning till evening all the tests were conducted and every report turned out to be normal but the pain would not subside. Even the doctors were surprised as they could not figure out where the problem was. Jyoti's worry grew with each passing hour seeing her husband suffer with unbearable pain. Then she suddenly remembered and sent her brother to the house to fetch UDI. It was evening then and the moment UDI was applied on his stomach, he felt off to sleep. Jyoti could feel the power of UDI and Baba's grace. She drew the curtain around the bed and stood outside there itself. In 5 mins a doctor came to visit him but Jyoti restricted the doctor, saying...

Abhi Abhi neend aayi hai, please sone dijiye

He has just slept, so please let him sleep

Meanwhile their son who is a devotee of Krishna was sitting in the house in front of the mandir and told Sai that if you do not help him then I will call my Krishna for help.

In a few minutes her husband woke up and called Jyoti inside. He said that two doctors just came and they put their hand on his stomach and now he is pain free. Jyoti was shocked as she was standing right outside the curtain and she did not allow anyone to enter, then how could any doctor visit. She immediately called her son who narrated his mother, how he requested Sai for help. Then joining the dots together, they realised that the two doctors were none other than Sai and Krishna. They had come to help him and relieved him of his pain. Later when they consulted the doctor, they got to know that it was a small 4 mm stone in his urinary track which was the cause of the pain. He was discharged and taken back home but the pain relapsed that night itself. The pain became unbearable and he pleaded for operation. But the doctors refused as it was too small a stone to be operated. There after whenever the pain aggravated UDI was applied on stomach and he would get relief and sleep. It continued this way for 4 days and then he got a final relief as the stone disappeared completely and he got permanent relief by the blessings of Sai's UDI.

Her faith in Baba grew immense and finally in August 2022 for the first time Jyoti visited Shirdi with her husband and both children. She was very excited to be in Sainagar as any ardent devotee of Baba would be. After completing the Dhoop Aarti, they (all three) were sitting outside Dwarkamai where she happened to meet a lady who coincidentally was from the same city Gurgaon, where Jyoti lived with her family currently. Both the ladies felt comfortable being from the same place and started talking to each other and shared grace of Baba merrily. Jyoti then told her about numerous miraculous incidents that happened in last one year and three months prior to coming Shirdi.

While they were talking and sharing experiences the lady told her something about her personal life which disturbed Jyoti very much and she chanted a silent prayer for her. While all this was happening, an old man came there from nowhere and asked Jyoti's husband to call her there. Her husband called her to come and meet him as he wanted to say something. Jyoti was very reluctant at the beginning but her husband consoled her that he was around and nothing would happen to her. He would keep a watch also. She went to the old man who in turn started walking away from the place where the entire family was sitting and asked Jyoti to follow him. She did but soon due to apprehension she told the old man...

'Whatever you have to say, say here only.'

The old man turned around and asked her to spread her palms. Initially she was hesitant but she did and to her pleasant surprise he placed many packets of 'UDI' in her palm. She was astonished and overwhelmed and was about to break in tears as it was her wish and demand from Baba that when she visits Shirdi she should get His darshan and lots of UDI. Her wish was just fulfilled by a stranger, the old man. In a trance she asked the old man.

Are you, my Baba?

But the old man said nothing, just smiled and lifted both his hands to shower blessings on all of them. Jyoti's tears did not stop realising and feeling the blessings of Sai. With smile on her face and tears of gratitude in her eyes they stood still there for a long time until they proceeded for their hotel.

She returned back to her husband and daughter in a state which she couldn't understand as she was crying with happiness of love and devotion towards her Sai. Baba had just fulfilled her desire, her request which she had made to him before coming to Shirdi. Her daughter took the Udi packets from her hand and counting them stated that there were 9 invaluable packets of UDI....This reminded Jyoti of her request to Baba ...

'I want your darshan and Lots of Udi when I go to Shirdi.'

They spent few days more in Shirdi and daily after Aarti she used to look for the same old man but he was never seen again.

Jyoti Mehta

Gurgaon
Mob : (+91) 9987942456
Email : pjyoti.mehta@gmail.com

17

BABA ACCEPTED DAKSHINA

In 1917 Haribhau Karnik of Dahanu (Thana District) came to Shirdi on the Guru-pournima day (in the month of Ashadha) and worshipped Baba with all formality. He offered clothes and Dakshina, and after taking Baba's leave through Shama, got down the steps of the Masjid. Then he thought that he should offer one more rupee to Baba and was just turning to get up when Shama informed him by signs that as he had got Baba's leave, he should go and not return. So he started for home. On his way, when he went into the temple of Kala Rama at Nasik for darshan, the Saint Narsing Maharaj who used to sit just inside the big door of the temple, left his Bhaktas there came to Haribhau, caught his wrist and said, 'Give me my one rupee'. Karnik was surprised. He paid the rupee most willingly and thought that Sai Baba recovered the rupee, which he intended in his mind to give, through saint Narsing Maharaj. Chapter XXXIII- Shri Sai Satcharita

Since Wednesday Baba was some way or the other hinting Moubani to visit Kali (Goddess) temple on Friday. She had a temple in her housing complex so she thought of visiting that on Friday. But Friday morning due to a lot of office work, she completely forgot all about visiting the Kali temple. Then she asked Baba some questions casually on question and answer website. Baba replied 'Feed the black dog'. Reading this instantly she remembered that Baba had prompted her to go to Kali temple the same day which she forgot. A thought came that she may visit the temple at night. But she got sad as the temple closes at 8 pm and she would not be able to reach the temple anyhow before 8:15 pm after finishing her office work. She felt sad and cursed herself on how she forgot to visit in the morning.

Still, after office she went to the mandir taking 11 rupees as Dakshina. Once she reached the temple, she got pleasantly shocked to see the mandir still open and the priest performing pooja, and few people were sitting there inside. She put the Dakshina in the Hundi and prayed to Ma Kali and was going back. Suddenly the priest called her and asked her to sit beside him. He was doing pooja and after completing that he applied red *Kumkum* on her forehead and blessed her by saying that soon she will get married. She was surprised as her parents were very worried for last 4 months because they couldn't find a suitable boy for her marriage. Words came true and she got engaged, married and settled abroad happily in USA.

Once on Baba's Day (Thursday), she went to the Sai temple to pray. While returning Sai gave her a thought of donating Rs. 20 to a beggar. She had little money in her purse but could donate 20 rupees. So happily, she stepped out of the temple to find one. But outside Baba's temple, there were so many beggars that if she would just give money to one out of so many, she would be *gheraoed* (encircled) by the rest to pay them as well. She got into a fix and sadly decided to let go of the idea to donate. Slowly she started walking towards her car which was parked at a distance. On reaching she saw just one beggar who was dressed and looked like Baba, who was sitting near her car only. On seeing her, the beggar spread his hand as if he was waiting for her to give him money. She got so happy and gave him Rs. 20.

Baba has his own ways ever since he was in His skin and bones to ask for Dakshina from his devotees and to fulfill their wishes.

Moubani Chatterjee
Kolkata
Mob : (+91) 9903856994
Email : moubani2011@gmail.com

18

QUENCH FOR DARSHAN

'In Shirdi many thoughts and ideas began to rise in your mind and I sent you here to rest your unsteady mind. You thought that I was in Shirdi with a body composed of the five elements and three and a half cubits in length, and not outside of it. Now you see and determine for yourself whether the person you see here now is the same you saw at Shirdi. It is for this reason that I sent you here.' Chapter XXXI - Shri Sai Satcharita

Sameer M Vaidya is an NRI working in Kuwait for long. He has been worshipping Shirdi Sai Baba since his college days when he was in India. Sameer vividly remembers the red color photograph of Baba in a steel frame kept in their house at Hyderabad. He used to visit the Saibaba temple near his house frequently when he was in India. When he was working in Jalna in Maharashtra, he used to visit Shirdi often and witnessed the divine Kakkad Aarti. Whenever he travels to India, he generally visits Shirdi Baba Temple either in Hyderabad, Bangalore or Chennai.

A few years ago in 2017, when he visited India, due to business he was not able to go to Shirdi Baba temple and was about to return to Kuwait from Mumbai. He was really sad about this but had no options as he had a return flight next morning. He was feeling really sad that he could not have darshan of Shirdi Baba during that trip. There he had put up in his aunt's house in Thane, West Mumbai. He asked his aunt if there was any Shirdi Baba Temple in the vicinity of their house. She told him that there was no Temple nearby but there was a garden with an idol of Saibaba under an open canopy.

Sameer was eager to have darshan so he took a quick bath and went to the garden with his cousin. He saw the marble Saibaba murthy (idol) under a canopy and did Pradakshina for about 30 minutes. Suddenly he saw a boy in his twenties with an aarti in his hand and chanting Mantras with great proficiency coming towards the Saibaba idol. He did the aarti to Baba's idol for about fifteen minutes while Sameer was standing and praying. Sameer was amused as he had never seen before such a wonderful aarti and heard such divine Mantras before. On closely observing the features of the boy, he got surprised. That boy perfectly resembled Saibaba idol from all angles. To double check he went around the idol and observed both the idol and the boy closely. He was amazed as there wasn't any doubt as both were matching from every direction and angle. He wondered how this could be true. Once the aarti and chanting got over that boy dressed in dark brown pants and cream shirt, offered the aarti to him and he went back into the dark in the opposite direction from where he came.

Sameer shared this unique Baba's experience with his friend's mother who was a staunch devotee of Shirdi Baba, and she said that since he was so desperate to have darshan of Sai Baba, He Himself came in the form of this young lad and gave darshan.

This demonstrates that Sai Baba is listening to all our thoughts, feelings, and emotions. Once again Baba proved us his omnipresence and omniscience.

Sameer M Vaidya
Kuwait
Mob : (00965)-65882972

19

MIRACULOUS DEBT RECOVERY

'Be wherever you like, do whatever you choose, remember this well that all what you do is known to Me. I am the Inner Ruler of all and seated in their hearts. I envelope all the creatures, the movable and immovable world. I am the Controller - the wirepuller of the show of this Universe. Chapter III – Shri Sai Satcharita

Once Suman Sharma a resident of Jaipur, Rajasthan was very tensed. She received a notice from her child's school for depositing school fee, without which the child would not be allowed to sit for the examination. She didn't have the money at that moment as she was jobless and was already burden with a lot of debts to repay. At that moment she was struggling to arrange daily ration for her house so she could not pay the school fees. If she couldn't pay the fees her child would lose 1 year because he wouldn't be allowed to sit for the exam. Since the time she received the notice, she kept on thinking how to arrange money but, was clueless as she couldn't find any avenues to arrange fund. For 3 days she kept crying and pleading to Baba to show her a way. But she didn't get any response or command from Baba. She started feeling hopeless until she remembered a money lender who could lend her money on interest. She gave him a phone call and had the following conversation: -

Suman (S): Hello Sir!!

Money lender (ML): Hello!! How come you called up today?

S: I need some money on interest.

ML: How much?

S: Rs. 7 to 8,000 to pay my child's school fee.

ML: Okay I will come to you tomorrow to talk and I will give you the money also. I like you very much and want to meet you, I want to be with you and spend some personal time with you.

The money lender was trying to exploit her taking advantage of her helpless situation. She got terrified and out of rage she hung up the phone and started sobbing again. She started cursing Baba and decided not to pray and follow Him anymore. Out of distress she lost all her faith in Baba and became absolutely impatient till Baba came up with a miracle. After a little while a gentleman, who owed her some money for a very long time of which she had forgotten, came up to her suddenly and handed over a cheque of Rs. 20,000. She was amazed at this Leela of Sai as she had already thought this to be a bad debt and suddenly when she was in dire need of money with no avenues open, Baba blessed her with her own money to meet up her crisis.

At times Baba stretches His devotees to such an extent that they lose faith in him. But we devotees need to understand Baba's all pervasiveness. He knows what his devotees' need and gives it to them at the correct moment.

A few words from Suman Ji for devotees...

Baba jaise aapne meri manokamna puri ki hai waise sab ki puri karna, aapka aashirvaad sab par yoon hi bana rahe, apna rahmo karam sab par banaye rakhna. Jaise aapne mujhe apna chamatkaar dikhaya hai waise hi sabko dikhana aur sab ka vishwas banaye rakhna.

Baba the way you have fulfilled my wishes, please do it for all the devotees. Keep showering your blessings on all of us like this. The way you have shown me this miracle, keep showing it to others also and let their faith remain intact.

Suman Sharma
Jaipur
Email : sumi101093@gmail.com

DEAL BLESSED BY BABA

Bhimaji Patil's prayer to God - 'Oh Lord Narayana, help me now'. It is a well-known fact that, when our circumstances are well off, we do not remember God, but when calamities and adversities over- take us, we are reminded of Him. Chapter XIII – Shri Sai Satcharita

Sharada who lives in Malapur, Karnataka was blessed by grace of Sai Baba and her life completely changed after that.

Sharada has an elder sister Sridevi who has sacrificed her entire life for the wellbeing of the family and was the main pillar of the family. Sharada's mamaji (maternal uncle) left behind a plot of land for them on his demise. Many years after passing away of Mamaji her sister decided to sell the plot of land because of weakening economic conditions of the family. Some of their relatives only agreed to buy the piece of land for a consideration of 50 lac rupees in total. They even gave an advance of rupees 14 lacs and balance to be paid on later dates. On receipt of advance Sridevi without any delay deposited the entire sum of 14 lacs as fixed deposit in Post office. But destiny had other plans and just after a few days the buyer of the land refused to go ahead with the deal and asked for his money back which he had given as advance. Sridevi was most worried as she didn't know what to do, how to return the money as it was already deposited in Post office schemes which have an inherent lock in period. Moreover, the entire family was shattered by the news of cancellation of deal as it was very important and required by them to live peacefully. Sharada the youngest member of the family was also deeply saddened by this and was wondering how will her sister manage to refund the money.

In worried state of mind, she went to Sai Baba temple and started praying to Baba to show her some way. She was standing in front of Baba with folded hands and a small girl came there and handed Sharadha a small book which was about Sai Baba *Vrat* (fasting) for 9 weeks. Sharada on turning the leaves of book, felt Baba himself had only sent this to her and resolved to do Sai Vrat for 9 weeks. She started her Vrat on a Thursday and performed it very religiously only wishing that Baba take them out of this trouble.

While Sharada was on 5th week of her Vrat, she heard a life changing news from the buyers of the plot of land wanted to continue with the deal, no longer did they want the advance back but will pay the remaining amount soon. Joys knew no bounds for Sharada and her family who were in difficult economic conditions found this sum of money would change their lives completely.

When Sai blessings are there, then there is no end to happiness and the same happened with Sharada and family who thereafter bought a new house for themselves from the money received and lived a happy and prosperous life thereafter.

Sharada. S
Malapur
Email : dishasha2000@gmail.com

21

SAI REMOVES HURDLES

Sai Baba often said that let His man (Devotee) be at any distance, a thousand koss away from Him, he will be drawn to Shirdi like a spar- row, with a thread tied to its feet. Chapter XXVIII – Shri Sai Satcharita

Sanjay ji is a Sai devotee for many decades now. And it is obvious that in such a long period of devotion he has gone through several miracles enjoying Baba's blessings. He has a treasure of knowledge about Sai literature and pictures in all these years. His articles have been published in 1980's in Sai Leela magazine. I personally call him an encyclopedia of Sai Baba and love to listen to his stories through his experiences and knowledge.

In June 1986, he and Sai brother Mr. Chandrakant Laha of Standard Chartered Bank drew up an itinerary to visit Shirdi on the auspicious occasion of 68th

Mahasamadhi day of Baba. But they revised their plan as it struck them that during that time Shirdi would be overcrowded and decided to go in September. It was the first trip to Shirdi for Chandrakant ji and they booked their tickets for 2 UP Mumbai mail scheduled to steam off from Howrah Station on 27 September, 1986. ... Little that they knew that the entire reschedule of trip was Leela of Baba.

Three days before the date of departure Calcutta, the 'City of Joy' received torrential rains which continued for 3 days making it a 'City of Sorrow'. Consequently, Sanjay ji could not contact Mr. Chandrakant as whether they could carry on with the scheduled visit and if yes how would they even reach Howrah Station. On 26 September, 1986 all hopes of visiting became bleak as the entire city was under 3 feet of water and there weren't any sign of rains stopping.

But to their surprise 27 September, 1986 began with a Sunny morning and the rain stopped. The water level came down on streets of Calcutta to a great extent. A few transport operators after 3 full days of lack of business ventured out on roads. This revived their spirits on 27th the day of departure and both of them met at State Bank of India, N.S. Road Branch to get some Traveller's Cheque. Initially the clerk was hesitant to issue tickets as trains didn't ply for last 3 days but on persuasion of Mr. Chandrakant, who himself was a banker, he did issue them citing the risk was theirs. Because they felt that trains would be cancelled or rescheduled from other platforms of Howrah Station, they left home early around 4.30 pm. By grace of Sai, it did not rain at all that day only a passing shower in afternoon and they reached Howrah Station safely.

At Howrah Station they realised many trains were cancelled or not plying and constant communication was made over the microphone. However only 2 trains were scheduled for departure including their Mumbai mail. Sai's grace manifested itself on that occasion and they were relieved to realise that Baba did want them to visit His Mausoleum at Shirdi. Though their train departed one hour late than scheduled at 9 pm but they reached their destination Nashik on time only at 3.40 am. That day they stayed there in Nashik and by Sai Baba grace could visit many important pilgrim spots.

On the morning of Tuesday 30th September, they reached Shirdi and thanked Baba for safe travel and even wrote letters to their home about their wellbeing and hassle-free journey. During the two and half days that they stayed at Shirdi. They performed abhishek to Baba's Samadhi very comfortably and in devout way. There they met many resident devotees during their stay and most noteworthy was meeting Baba Maartand.

Thus, by the grace of Baba their journey was completed without any trouble whereas it was looking impossible when they started. It was certainly a miracle by Baba.

Jai Sai Ram

Sanjay M Padiya

Kolkata

Mob : (+91) 98368 10104

22

SAI-MAA

Baba said to Dixit, 'Tell him to be fearless. Why should he suffer for ten births? In ten days he can work out the sufferings and consequences of his past Karma. While I am here to give him temporal and spiritual welfare.' Chapter XXXIV - Shri Sai Satcharita

Megha is a Sai devotee from Bangalore and has been connected to Sai Baba since her childhood as her mother is devoted to Sai for many years.

Megha narrates...

'I always got that motherly love from Baba. Sometimes strict, most of the times he is epitome of love.'

It was way back 2020 and Megha retired early for the night after a very tiring day. At the middle of the night suddenly, she starting getting cough and it struck her nose and throat so hard that she couldn't breathe. Megha was alone with no one at that moment by her side. She was struggling to breathe. Her breathlessness made her feel restless and she started moving her hand and legs in despair. She felt as if she would die of breathlessness. Suddenly she felt someone held her right arm. Megha became almost senseless. She did not bother to open her eyes to check who it was, such was the state of pain she was going through. But she could feel a warm big palm and 5 long fingers holding on to her right arm. This did not last long. Like a flash of a moment in a few seconds, Megha started breathing normally.

Megha narrates..

'When I got back to my senses and I turned on lights, I was surprised to see UDI on my right arm...'

It was none other than Baba who came there and held her hand and saved her. Megha and her entire family have been Baba's Devotees for a very long time. Her grandmother used to say...

'No other paraphernalia is needed, just love SAI in every form. This is the only way to get him and Baba will love you hundred folds back'

After this incident Megha personally felt his motherly love. She always thanks Baba for showering His motherly love upon her and giving her such a loving family, where everyone has immense love and devotion towards Baba.

Megha is always grateful to Baba for everything in her life.

Meghna S Rao
Bangalore
Email : meghanasrao11@gmail.com

23

SEPERATION AVERTED

Baba's Advice Regarding our Behaviour

The following words of Baba are general and invaluable. If they are kept in mind and acted upon, they will always do you good. 'Unless there is some relationship or connection, nobody goes anywhere.' If any men or creatures come to you, do not discourteously drive them away, but receive them well and treat them, with due respect. Shri Hari (God) will be certainly pleased. Chapter XVIII and XIX – Shri Sai Satcharita

'Ok. Text me your final choice, Motorazor or Nokia' texted Mahesh as he sat in Nashik airport in 2010, April. 'No Mahesh. You don't have to give me anything. It's perfectly fine' Shobana texted back.

'So, see you on Saturday for lunch. I shall confirm the venue soon. Surely, it will be somewhere near our office' texted back Mahesh. He was pretty sure of not being recognized in that area, and he was sure that his wife doesn't know the place around, so that seemed like a safe bet, given the circumstances.

'Alright' came the reply from Shobana.

Mahesh worked as an operations head in a leading multinational, and Shobana worked as his secretary for the last 5 years. Their daily interactions in close proximity had brought them closer with each passing day. For the last one year, Shobana had started sharing her personal issues with Mahesh, who in turn discussed them with his wife Mahati. Shobana had slowly transformed from a colleague to a family friend. Mahesh was aware that she had a strained relationship with her businessman husband and she was supporting all his needs as well as the needs of her daughter aged 12. Mahesh never realised when he had developed a special feeling towards Shobana. Initially, he thought he was helping her out, but as days passed by, he realised what he felt for her was more than care.

Mahesh was married for the last 10 years to beautiful and well-educated Mahati who hailed from an illustrious family. After his marriage to Mahati, he had witnessed a meteoric rise in his profession, which had led them to lead a very comfortable living. He openly admitted that Mahati was indeed his lucky mascot. They were blessed with a boy, who was now an eight-year-old. Overall, theirs was a happy go lucky family.

'Last call for boarding' announced the ground staff as Mahesh bid a final bye to Shobana. He closed the text messages, and as a regular habit, he dialed a call to Mahati, his wife. 'I am boarding now. I hope Vicky is back from school' he said.

'Oh wow! that's nice' came Mahati's sweet voice from the other side. 'Yes, he is back and is eagerly waiting to have you back home.' Mahesh's incessant travels to different parts of India, kept him away from home for long intervals. 'I hope you have a safe flight, see you soon,' she said. 'Yes, see you soon 'Mahesh disconnected the call as he settled down comfortably in his seat.

'Am I not wrong.? What has Mahati done to me that I am drawn towards Shobana. Mahati has been a very dutiful and loving wife, always' his mind was now up to some comparison. 'Is Shobana prettier than Mahati? No. Is she more educated and confident than Mahati? No' he could just not find the answer. He also pretty well knew Mahati was an excellent wife, mom, daughter and daughter in law and did all her responsibilities towards them all. Then what was it that was drawing him to Shobana? he did not have the answer himself. Probably, the excess of money that Mahesh was seeing in this phase of his life lead him here.

Mahati on the other hand, could sense some changes in her husband's behaviour. He had recently become inseparable from his phone, which slightly lead her to suspect something fishy. Just a fortnight ago, her friend had casually informed Mahati, that she saw Mahesh and Shobana in Shopper's Stop. 'Yes, I know, he did go there. He picked up some clothes for the three of us' Mahati had replied to her friend in the most unsuspecting manner. But, she had never in her wildest dreams imagined what she was staring at.

'Vicky has a match this Saturday', she informed her husband.

'I may not be able to come Mahati. I have an important meeting to attend' Mahesh could not meet his wife's eyes.

'What meeting on a weekend' Mahati prodded further.

'Now, do I have to inform you about the minutest things I do? Mahesh was visibly upset, but staring away. 'I have committed to meeting some old friends' he said.

'Alright' said Mahati. By now, she clearly knew something was fishy.

The next morning, Mahesh headed to shower and Mahati opened his phone without his knowledge. As she opened the text messages, her hand shivered as she read the exchange of messages between Mahesh and Shobana. She blacked out for a minute, held the wall next to her as a support and collapsed on her bed. In less than a minute, she composed herself and headed straight to the kitchen. She packed his lunch mechanically, as she started visualizing her family break into bits.

The moment Mahesh stepped out to his office, Mahati rushed to the pooja room and held her Baba's statue in her hand. She took it near her heart and broke into inconsolable sobs. She almost felt her heart tearing into pieces. She shuddered at the thought of the insecure future of herself and Vicky. 'Baba do you think I deserve the pain I am going through now. If u think so, so be it' she spoke to her Baba. 'You will be responsible for Vicky's life and mine' she said as she continued sobbing inconsolably. There was no one to console her and neither could she share this incident with anyone. She spent the whole day crying.

Saturday Mahesh accompanied her to Vicky's match, but she saw that he was continuously on his phone. 'Probably a new lunch date is being worked out', Mahati's heart sank and her throat choked. The couple got ready to head out to a dinner that evening, upon Mahesh's insistence. Vicky was at a friend's house for a sleepover. It was night, back at home but Mahesh was still restless and he informed Mahati that the meeting with his friend was postponed to the next day, not knowing that Mahati by now knew who that friend was.

'Give me 5 minutes' she told her husband. 'I urgently need some groceries for tomorrow morning. I shall fetch it from the neighborhood store.' she pretended to go out, but just went and stood in the guest room. In less than a minute, she could hear Mahesh's voice 'Yes Shobana, don't worry about the car. Tell me which one you want; you can take any of my three cars. My driver will drop it off at your house tomorrow morning' he said.

Mahati stepped out of the guest room, went straight to her pooja room, opened the box of UDI which she had got with her, applied on her forehead and walked straight to her bedroom. Mahesh was still on the phone. 'See you tomorrow and bye for now' he said and turned back to see Mahati right behind him.

'I am completely aware of everything Mahesh' she said. He was surprised with the composure she exhibited. 'You will be completely free from my clutches, if you feel you want to continue your relationship with Shobana. But one thing is for sure, you cannot be travelling on two ships at the same time' her voice was feeble but firm.

It was Mahesh's turn to stay stunned, he had been caught red handed and confronted.

'Why are you imagining things?' he retorted, Mahati cut him short. 'I have read all your conversations with Shobana, before you deleted them all.'

Mahesh was completely helpless, and he had nothing to say in his defense. 'Believe me Mahati. We have not gone anywhere beyond a few lunch meetings' Mahesh could barely recognize his meek voice. He had no option, but to surrender. 'Can I have your phone?' she asked and Mahesh handed it over to her, as if he was being cast by a spell. The next thing she did was to dial Shobana's number. 'Hello Mahesh' said Shobana 'Yes, we definitely are meeting tomorrow' Mahati paused for a moment. She had put the mobile on speaker and Mahesh could barely face his wife. He put his neck down in shame having admitted his mistake. 'It is me Mahati here Shobana' said Mahati in a firm tone. 'I want to meet you in the next one hour. I am now coming to your house.'

'Can we have some privacy please?' said Mahati, as Shobana walked inside and sat in their car parked in front of Shobana's house. Mahesh got down from the car and walked in the opposite direction.

'Shobana, so far, I have helped you during all times of distress, and is this what I get in return? Mahati looked straight into Shobana's eyes. 'Believe me Mahati. I do not have any role to play here. I have had enough from my husband that I cannot even think of getting into any other relationship. It was Mahesh who kept on pestering me to go out with him and he was the one who would call me always' said Shobana as tears welled up in her eyes. Mahati clearly knew she was lying. 'I did see a few incoming calls on Mahesh's number from your hand phone Shobana' said Mahati. 'He is my boss and I do have to return his calls Mahati, try to understand' said Shobana trying her level best to prove her innocence.

Now, Mahati called Mahesh back to the car and made them sit in front of each other. 'Shobana says you were the one pestering her to go out, much against her will Mahesh. What do u have to say to this now?' asked Mahati directly. Mahesh looked unbelievably into Shobana's face now 'Shobana, I accept that I did call. You were the one who promptly answered my calls, replied to all messages and encouraged me to keep doing it' he said. 'You were my boss. I didn't have any option, did I' she asked. Mahesh could not believe his ears. 'Okay it's a final good bye Shobana, he said.' He was being punished from both sides for his fault. He had realised a hard way that he ran behind a piece of glass leaving behind a crystal he owned.

Mahati was crying inconsolably, as they headed back home. Mahesh had no words to console her, he was completely ashamed and guilty. 'I promise Mahati, this was the first and last chance you got to complain against me. I will promise you that it will not repeat.' Mahesh said as he hugged his wife reassuringly.

The couple stood in Dwarkamai a fortnight later, with Mahesh's transfer order in hand. He had been promoted and transferred to Dubai. Mahati stood in front of her Baba, as she thanked him profusely for bringing this extra marital affair to her notice before it could cause a major damage to their marriage. Her unstinted faith in Baba stood the test of times once again.

Baba had guarded his devotee yet again!

Om Sai Ram

Anonymous Devotee

24

CORONA CURED

I am the mother - origin of all beings - the Harmony of three Gunas, the propeller of all senses, the Creator, Preserver and Destroyer. Nothing will harm him, who turns his attention towards Me. Chapter III – Shri Sai Satcharita

Soniya Deorukhkar is a Baba's devotee for long residing in Mumbai. In the year 2021 when the 2nd brutal wave of COVID-19 broke in July, situation was terrible in India. There were no beds available with shortage of oxygen and medicines. During that period Soniya and her entire family, her daughter and husband all got into the clutches of the deadly Corona. Soniya is an asthma patient suffered more than a normal human being. On getting the COVID positive result, the entire family started with medication at home. All other than Soniya started recovering after taking medicines for 3 days but her health started deteriorating because of breathlessness due to low oxygen levels.

3rd day was Thursday, when in the morning around 11 am her condition became extremely critical as she could not breathe. They all were praying to Baba for help to recover. Soniya was extremely worried for her family more than for her as she could sense that her life was coming to an end. During the second wave she had known so many cases when the victim was admitted to hospital but never came back. Hence, she ruled out the choice of going to hospital also. Her heart started sinking as she could not figure out what to do. She was not able to talk, breath, or even stand. She thought that her game got over.

But Baba and his miraculous ways always work instantly for his choice of devotees. It was Soniya and her entire family who got Baba's blessings. She has a brother, who at times comes to her home but never comes without calling them, who arrived that afternoon from Mira Road directly without intimation. He stood at the door as they didn't allow him in, because of the chances of catching infection. From outside itself by talking to them he understood the emergency of the situation and pleaded with them for immediate hospitalization. Again and again till 2 pm he tried to convince her for admission to hospital but Soniya did not agree. When he lost his patience he shouted in so loud voice...

> *Marna hai kya tujhe? Zid chod de, chali Jaa, Tera baba bhi wahi hoga tere saath*
>
> Do you want to die? Don't be stubborn, Go to the hospital. You will find your Baba there also

Hearing this she was full of tears. When she looked up to her brother, she could see Baba's Swaroop in him who was shouting at her like anything. She lost her senses and just gazed at Baba. She could see the Halo around his head and his arms which were calling her to take her to the hospital. Finally, they all agreed. Finding a bed in the hospital was the most challenging thing to do without a source of an official those days. With Baba's grace they instantly got confirmation of a bed in a hospital in Andheri over a phone call. Only 3 beds were left and they were exactly 3 of them for admission. Time was running out as the situation was critical. Ambulance was requested from the hospital. If the ambulance would have come from Andheri to her house at Borivali it would take a long time. But it was Baba's grace that the hospital ambulance at that critical moment was in the next lane and it came to pick them in no time.

Soniya's situation was extremely critical due to breathlessness. There was no oxygen in the store then. Chances of Soniya's survival was very low without oxygen. They were all worried on how to arrange oxygen, but Baba has all plans ready. A lady on another bed next to Soniya had just recovered from corona and had an oxygen cylinder. On sensing the emergency, she asked doctor...

> *Iss ko oxygen lagaoo nahi toh yee marjayi gii, mera oxygen nikalo main ab thik huu*

> I am fine now. Take out my oxygen and put it on her else she will die

The doctor was surprised hearing such a humanitarian act and then they put her on oxygen immediately. Remdesivir Injection which was required immediately to save her was not available then. Another blessing of Sai that at late night someone gave 6 injections to nurse pointing at Soniya and saying...

> *Meri maa ab thik hai, inko jaroorat hai please inko de dijiye.*

> My mother is fine now; she needs it so give it to her

Everything kept happening on its own and Soniya was shocked with each thing happening so easily. She started crying uncontrollably feeling Baba's grace. A nurse came then and hugged her tight saying...

> *Baba aapke saath hai aaj. Aaj Saivaar hai. Daro mat. Aap, aapki beti aur aapke pati sab thik hoker 7/8 dino main ghar chale jaaooge*

Baba is there with you. Today is a Thursday. Do not worry. You along with your daughter and husband will recover and go back home in 7/8 days.

Second day inspite of oxygen and medications she was feeling worse as her breathing became more difficult. She started crying as she could sense that she was dying. She felt asleep while crying and saw dream in which Baba was sitting next to her bed saying

> *Kuch kha lo aacha lagega aur tumhe aathve din Ghar jaane miljaayega daroo mat. Main yahi huu, tumhe kuch hua toh meri seva kon karega beta*

> Eat something then you will feel good. Do not fear as you will be allowed to return home on 8th day. I am right here with you. If anything happens to you then who will give me service my child

And he hugged her tight, and slept in his white dress beside her bed on the ground and water started flowing under Baba. She slept peacefully for hours and when she woke up her oxygen levels had improved like anything and she was hungry. She ate fruits then, as advised by Baba and recovered absolutely within 6th day, and they discharged her on the 8th day which was also *Saivaar* (Thursday).

Sai is miraculous and he has his ways and is always there to help and protect us.

Sonia Deoukhkar
Mumbai
Email : soniyadeorukhkar73@gmail.com

25

MIRACLE OF 9 WEEKS VRAT

The following words of Baba are general and invaluable. If they are kept in mind and acted upon, they will always do you good. 'Unless there is some relationship or connection, nobody goes anywhere. If any men or creatures come to you, do not discourteously drive them away, but receive them well and treat them, with due respect. Shri Hari (God) will be certainly pleased. It is on account of Rinanubandh (former relationship) that we have come together, let us love and serve each other and be happy.' Chapter XVIII and XIX – Shri Sai Satcharita

Resident of Dinhata, in the district of Cooch Behar, West Bengal, Roma Roy is a dedicated devotee of

Lord Sai who has blessed her with many miraculous incidents, out of which she narrates a few....

Roma came to know Baba in 2018. Her husband who was previously married to other women was very disturbed those days. Though he had love marriage with his first wife that lady was not good to him as well as his family which disturbed his entire life. The lady made his life miserable and when he wanted divorce from her, she didn't even accept that. He (Roma's husband) was a very simple loving person by nature and could not tolerate this non peaceful environment at home and decided to take divorce from the lady, ie. The first wife.

From the year 2013 both Roma and her husband used to work in the same Courts and hence knew each other well. Roma's husband used to share his stories with Roma which saddened her a lot and she felt very bad for him. She used to worship Maa Bipatarani Chandi (Goddess) every Tuesday during those days and used to visit temple every Tuesday. One day she cried a lot in front of goddess to show her some way she could help her husband to get rid of the mischievous lady.

In 2017, one day while watching TV she came across the serial *'Mere Sai'* through which she got attracted towards Sai. She then decided to perform

Pooja of Sai Baba. But now the challenge was that she hardly knew anything about Sai Baba and wanted to know and learn more about him. She searched the Facebook app and there a girl told her some details regarding the same. It was in March 2018 Roma had come to Kolkata for some reason and there she bought a small idol of Sai Baba. But somehow, she couldn't start the process of worshipping the Lord at that time. One night in her dream appeared a saint exactly dressed like Sai Baba. She held His feet and wept. She prayed to Sai that she wanted to worship him. Her dream broke and she realized that it was Thursday, Baba's Day, but still couldn't start her Pooja as desired.

Later in August 2020 she started performing rituals of Sainath and started a 9 weeks Sai Vrat with the desire that her husband gets free from his existing wife who was unwilling to come to mutual separation hence there was a case going on in the court of law. Miracles of Baba started taking place in Roma's life, her desires started getting fulfilled as the lady who was contesting the case in court of law suddenly decided to withdraw from it and hence Roma's husband won the case of divorce. This twist was no less than a miracle in Roma's and her husband's life. Later he also won the case of maintenance which normally goes in favor of opposite party.

Indian marriages are expensive affairs and she was wondering how would she take care of all single handedly and was deeply worried. She sincerely requested Baba to take care of everything which by his grace worked out smoothly. She wanted the presence of Baba during her marriage and it happened as she could feel Baba during all rituals and ceremonies and she was extremely happy with all miracles happening in her life.

Roma's husband didn't believe in God much. Suddenly his Mama fell seriously ill and doctors raised the white flag saying he wouldn't survive for more than 24 hours in state of coma. She earnestly prayed for Baba's mercy on her husband's Mama to cure him. With divine blessings he did get out of danger and thus her husband's faith in Sai Baba consolidated.

Roma had numerous miraculous incidents and she now sees and lives Baba every breath of her life and swears by grace of Sai Baba.

Om Sai Ram

Roma Roy

Cooch Behar
Mob : (+91) 7384421836

26

HEALING JOURNEY

The most effective and speedy way to gain our object is to approach a worthy Saint or Sage - Sadguru, who has himself attained God-vision. Sai Baba was such a Sage or Sad-Guru. Though He acted as a Fakir (mendicant), He was always engrossed in the Self. He always loved all beings in whom He saw God or Divinity. Chapter VIII – Shri Sai Satcharita

Basant Kumar Palai is a resident of Jharsuguda, Orissa, by profession a teacher running a tutorial taking Math and Physics classes.

Everyone goes through ups and downs in life. So was the same with the Palai family when Mrs. Palai went through serious health problems in March 2007. Basant initially took it causally but his wife's condition started worsening which worried him a lot. He went to a number of doctors but no improvement was there in his wife's health condition. Rather day by day she was getting worse and started avoiding food due to which she became weak. Their son and daughter both were very young school going children. Gradually she became weak and was unable to perform her daily routine work. So, it became really difficult for Basant to manage the children, his work and essential work at home. He was really worried and shared his concern with family and friends. A friend named Rabi Nair who was a Sai devotee asked him to go to Shirdi and seek Baba's blessings. Basant was a religious person but did not know much about Sai Baba. On hearing miracle stories from his friend, he agreed to go to Shirdi in June 2007. Soon tickets were booked. But by then her condition had worsened drastically and all his neighbours advised him for immediate hospitalization. He kept faith and left all on Baba and started his journey along with his and Rabi's family on 5th June by an afternoon train. It was a very hot day and they were waiting for the train at the Jharsuguda railway station.

Miracles started then and from there only. He offered Cold drinks to everyone and at the same time asked his wife too. She agreed. 'I gave her frooty and she took it comfortably,' said Basant. He got so happy that at least she drank something. Then he gave snacks to everyone as it was lunchtime and all were hungry. 'She also asked me to give her the snacks' narrates Basant. Mrs. Palai was not eating and drinking anything for a few days now and this incident brought joy leaps and bounds in Basant's heart. He couldn't imagine that she would eat anything and this itself gave a lot of strength to Basant as he started witnessing miracles even before reaching Shirdi. They boarded the train and throughout the journey she ate and drank which contented his heart and got eager to reach Shirdi. After a very long time he saw his wife in deep sleep and in the next morning they arrived at Manmad. Mrs. Palai was in a much better condition by then. Everyone was shocked with such a drastic improvement as Baba had started showering his blessings. They finally arrived in Shirdi at 11:45am and stayed there for 8 days visiting nearby places like Nashik, Aurangabad, Shani Shignapur etc. Basant narrates...

'After coming from Shirdi I took her to Dr. Dubey - one of the senior most doctor of our area.'

He said

Sabse Bada Doctor Ka haath Jab tumhare Sath tab mere kya jarurat!

When the biggest doctor of the Universe is with you, then where am I required

Dr. confirmed Basant that his wife was perfectly fine, and there is nothing to be done.

Till today she is fine and never had any such health issues.

Basant Kumar Palai
Jharsuguda
Mob : (+91) 9439401845

27

CONNECT DIRECTLY – SAID SAI

The last wish or thought that a man has at the hour of death, determines his future course. Shri Krishna has said in Gita (VIII-5-6) that 'he who remembers Me in his last moments, comes verily to Me, and he that meditates otherwise at that time goes to what he looks for.' We cannot be certain that we can entertain a particular good thought at our last moment, for, more often than not, we are more likely to be frightened and terrified by many causes. Hence constant practice is necessary for enabling us to fix our mind on any desired good thought at any or the last moment. All Saints, therefore, recommended us to always remember God and chant His name, so that we may not be puzzled when the time for departure comes. The devotees on their part surrender themselves completely to the Saints, fully believing that the all-knowing Saints would guide and help them in their last moments. Chapter XXXI - Shri Sai Satcharita

It was a Thursday 10 September, 2020, when Pooja was reading Shri Sai Satcharita while her mobile rang. Pooja a staunch devotee of Sai from Delhi picked up the phone anxiously. It was her mother's call from Indore. She broke the news of her grandmother passing away. Pooja immediately broke into tears as she was very close to her grandmom. She got consoled by the following words from her mom…

'When Maa left for heavenly abode, she had UDI in her hand. I was reading Satcharita and your brother was with his Guruji.' Pooja had Satcharita in her hand too that moment. It was a Thursday and since everyone at that moment was somehow or the other connected to Sai, Pooja understood that it was Sai who came and gave salvation to her Grandmom. Hence, she could console herself and got at ease.

Sai gives the pain and has his own ways to heal them also somehow or the other. It is a well-known fact amongst all Sai devotees that Sai Satcharita has answers to all our questions and has its own ways to cool down all storms which arise in our lives. Such was the affair with Pooja as the chapters which she was allotted consoled her completely.

Pooja narrates...

'Mujhe wahi chapters mile jisme Baba ji ne udi ki mahima samjhate hue bataya hai ki, ye sharir kewal ek raakh ki tarah hai, jo ki hame UDI hamesha samjhati hai. Jaise Baba mujhe condolence de rahe ho aur samjha rahe ho, jiski wajah se mujhe shanti mil rahi ho and madad ho rahi ho us jhatke se nikalne mein.'

I was allotted those chapters which explained the glory of UDI, that the body is one which has emerged from ash and will merge into ash, like the UDI. It was as if Baba is consoling her through the reading which helped her to get out that shock.

This wasn't enough. It was the brutal 2nd wave of COVID-19 which was going on at that time and Pooja couldn't go to Indore for the last rites. She was extremely anxious as she wanted to have at-least a last darshan of her lovely Grandma who was like mother Yashoda to her. She pleaded Sai to help her. She slept pleading Sai and next morning she saw a dream...

She saw, there was a room in which 3 other persons are sitting in white dress. They had very glowing faces as angels. One boy got her there in the room where her grandmom was also entering, wearing a saree (Indian dress). She looked so young and happy with a very high glow on her face. Pooja tried calling her but the boy said that she cannot listen. 'You can only see her' the boy told Pooja in her dream. Pooja perplexed in her dream asked the boy, *'Are U Sai?'* The boy smiled towards her and the dream got over.

Pooja woke up to realise that it was a dream but got happy that she could see her grandmom. Later during the day her mother shared a picture of the last rites. Looking at the picture Pooja was taken aback as it was the same saree which she was wearing which Pooja had seen her grandmom wearing in the dream. Pooja got doubly confirmed that it was Sai who took her with him.

And also, it doesn't end here. Next day she again saw her grandmother in her dream. In the dream some function was going on in their house which Grandma also attended but other than Pooja no one could see or talk to her.

'Grandma tell me if it was Sai who took you away?' asked Pooja

She replied- 'I do not know who it was but I know this that when I was given UDI, I felt very calm and peaceful and now I am feeling very happy.'

Now here the Baba's Leela...

When she was conversing with her grandma, in her dream, she felt as if Baba came near her bed and scolded her for not trusting and asking him directly. Sai further said that

'I had shown you last night that she is with me, then why can't you believe and trust me. If you have any questions, why don't you ask me directly?'

In Sai Satcharita also Sai has asked devotees to connect directly with them. Pooja narrates...

'I felt so sorry that day and asked Baba to forgive me. Thereafter I have decided in my life to have only one to one conversation with Baba.'

How lovely our Baba is... love you so much Sai.

Pooja Chadha

Delhi
Mob : (+91) 96466 10725
Email : pooja20247@gmail.com

28

UNIVERSAL SAI

Sai Baba is always full of mercy. What is wanted on our part is whole-hearted devotion to Him. When a devotee has got firm faith and devotion, his wishes are soon fulfilled. Chapter XXV Shri Sai Satcharita

Anu an ardent Sai devotee who lives in USA has deep faith in Sai and this belief is purely due to series of miracles that have taken place in her life back from 2017. Having born in city of Delhi in a religious family, she values humanity and life on a whole. Her gratitude towards Sai is reinforced on a daily basis through the preaching's of Shraddha and Saburi.

Anu, by virtue of being born in a religious family used to worship many Hindu deities but did not know about Sai till her marriage. She moved out of Delhi in June 2001 after her marriage and stayed in many cities in India and abroad. During one of their relocations, they moved to Mumbai and visited Shirdi for the first time in 2004 with some friends. Thereafter, they visited Shirdi several times from Mumbai, not out of pure devotion but like any other weekend getaway.

During one of their visits in 2010 on their way back to Mumbai from Shirdi, their car brakes failed. With great difficulty, her husband managed to stop the car with the help of the handbrake, and they were stranded on the roadside with their two small kids. Suddenly a car stopped in front of them, and a man came out and offered help. What help could be more than a lift at that moment. He dropped them at a nearby hotel, and after guiding them, went his way. It's quite common in India that no one gives lift to a stranger. This man had also not done the same before this incident. He told them *'Sai had sent me for your help.'* Both Anu and her husband were quite overwhelmed by this experience and thanked him and Sai a lot, but after coming back home, got busy with their lives and did not connect much with Sai.

Anu narrates...

'I often prayed to the Almighty to send me a Guru in my life, and Sainath was the answer to my prayers.'

Anu moved to Hyderabad in 2017. There her younger daughter started watching the series of

'Mere Sai' which gets telecast every weekday at 7pm IST on Sony Liv TV channel. Anu started watching it too along with her daughter. Sai made inroads in their lives through that serial, and they got engrossed into it and slowly started connecting with Him.

Then one day Anu's younger daughter, by mistake, spilt a glass full of water on her elder one's MacBook (laptop). The keyboard got completely soaked, and the MacBook conked off instantly. Similar instance had happened while they were in Singapore and this MacBook was a replacement of that incident. The younger one started crying profusely as her sister started scolding her. It was late in the night and Anu being their mother had to console them both. She then asked her younger one to pray to Sai to make it work again and then go off to sleep. Her younger daughter cried and prayed in front of Baba and kept the MacBook under the fan and slept. On waking up in the morning, they found it working perfectly, and were truly amazed at Sai's Leela. Anu expressed her immense gratitude to HIM, and after this incident, Sai had carved HIS place in her life. Anu said

'I knew that my Guru had entered my life.'

Many miracles happened with Anu after that, and the following one is one of the most noteworthy. Anu along with her family moved to Chicago, USA in

August 2019 owing to her husband's work, for three years. Her faith in Sai was growing stronger, and she started connecting much better with Him. During covid times, in March-April 2020, a cousin of Anu sent her a link to join Global Mahaparayan group. (Reading of Shri Sai Satcharita). She felt so grateful towards her cousin and instantly joined the group. Shri Sai Satcharita completely changed her life, and helped her delve deeper into the life of her dear Sai, as she started reading it religiously. Anu started experiencing Sai's miracles and she started communicating with Sai. Prior to Sai Anu used to follow Nirgun Brahma (formless God) and from there her life transformed to a Sagun Brahma - Her Sai (God with an Idol). Each passing day her devotion increased in Sai.

By the grace of Sai all settled soon in USA and both her daughter's got admission in good schools there. Anu was very happy as everything got settled there quickly. Her elder daughter had to take admission in college next year so Anu was keen to have their USA visa extended as she wanted to stay closer to her daughter. But the US job role for her husband was until June, 2022. Anu kept praying to Sai to help him find a new role in his organization so that their US visa's got extended. She kept praying to Sai with full Shraddha and Saburi (faith and patience) to help them. Anu used to recite *'Sai Baba ke 11 vachan'* (eleven promises of Sai Baba), and two of them always stays in her consciousness. Anu narrates

'Sometimes when I woke up in the middle of the night, I would feel the following two *vachans* (promises) continually going on in my head' -

Mann mein rakhna dridh vishwas, kare samaadhi poori aas

My tomb shall bless and speak to the needs of my devotees

Meri sharan aa khaali jaaye, ho koi to mujhe bataaye

Is there anyone who has come to my tomb and not received my blessings

When Anu was a child, her father used to always say with conviction ...

Beta bhagwaan se maango, pray karo, woh sab dete hain

Child, ask God what you want, pray to Him, He will answer all your prayers

And now Anu started to pray to Sai, her God.

She used to talk to Sai and say,

Main jitni prayers kar sakti thi, maine ki, jo bhi insights aap ne di, unhe follow kiya

I have prayed as much as I could, whatever insights you gave me, I followed them

Not out of any desperation but out of *bhakti* (devotion)... 'If my prayers are still not answered, I will never be able to tell my children with the same conviction that a sincere prayer from the heart can move mountains, and help achieve the impossible in our lives.'

Anu used to eat, drink, sleep, and breathe her prayers to Sai to help her husband find a new job role in his organization, and get their US visa extended. She got so much strength from His devotion that she never worried, and kept faith and patience, and completely surrendered to Him. Her teachings to her children were:

'Replace your worry with a prayer.'

She also took a vow that she will not eat Mango (her favourite fruit) and cookies (her favourite munchie with tea), and told Sai that she will have them only after He answered her prayers, and called her to Shirdi to thank Him. All along, she kept asking Sai for signs to show her that He was listening to her prayers.

So, she got her first sign from Him in January 2021. She is a part of a global Mahaparayan, and she used to get many links of miracles that happened with people while doing the parayaan. One day, she just casually clicked on a link out of so many, and read the miraculous account of a lady who had been trying for her Canadian visa but failed multiple times. This was the last time she was trying with virtually no hope. She was constantly praying to Sai, and finally got it. Anu took it as her sign that they will get their visa too!

A few more weeks passed and nothing seemed to move. Anu's anxiety started increasing as there wasn't much time left. Sai had given her a signal earlier but nothing actually had happened yet. So, she prayed to Sai again to show her another sign. In March 2021, Sai gave her a dream. In her dream, her both daughters and Anu were on a flight to India. The flight was still boarding, and she was waiting for her husband to board. He came in and whispered in her ear

'Ho gaya' (it's done).

Anu's dream broke with joy to realise that it was just a dream. But she got satisfied through this dream that her husband will get a new job role, but at the last minute, and she was to follow His path of Shraddha and Saburi (faith and patience).

There was still time for them to move back to India but anxiety would keep soaking in at times. By now her elder daughter had got admission in a very good university, and Anu wanted to stay close to her, there in USA itself. Anu through her previous two signs believed that her prayers will surely be heard and her work will be done but anxiety won't stop. She still kept asking for signs from Sai. Then HE gave her a third sign in August 2021. One day as soon as she opened Facebook, she got a picture of Sai which read that the job they were praying for, would happen soon. Her joy had no bounds, and she cried with joy remembering the teachings of Sai to keep Shraddha and Saburi.

Anu and her husband both took up a vow to do 9 weeks of Sai Vrat, offered Sai water, food, prayers, etc. every day, and also read Shri Sai Satcharita. Kids also prayed with full faith. Several times, it seemed like her husband almost got a new job role but due to some or other reasons there were delays and even by 2nd week of May 2022, no new role in the US had been finalized. Their USA visa was till June 9, 2022. Logically by then they had to vacate the house and prepare for return. They gave notice to their landlord, packers and movers were intimated, and the mobility team in her husband's office started liaising and preparing for their repatriation back to India. Her husband was still trying to find another role in the US but nothing had materialised so far. She did not lose her faith and patience in Sai but still began to prepare to move back. The date of departure from the US to India was fixed as June 8, 2022 just a day before the expiry of their Visa.

The return to India seemed inevitable. Her elder daughter came back to them from her university during her holidays and booked tickets to one 'Tulip farm' for a weekend on May 14, 2022. Anu asked her husband to take them to the nearby Sai temple in the morning on their way to the tulip farm. He instantly agreed but unfortunately, they got late in the morning. They had to reschedule their mandir visit after tulip farm as the mandir was already closed by then. Anu kept her prayers on and kept asking Sai for one last sign that her prayers would be fulfilled - that her husband would get a new job role in his organization, and their US visa would get extended. The trip to the farm went well, and they sat back in the car to head towards Sai temple. Her heart was throbbing all time asking for one last sign from Sai that HE would grant her wish. When seated in the car, her husband asked her to open google map to locate Sai temple. She just casually opened Google (not google maps), and searched for 'Sai temple near me.' Suddenly she saw that the nearest Sai temple was labelled as 'Visa temple of Sai Baba.' She was totally stunned as she had never before heard of the Visa temple of Sai Baba. On checking the address, her husband reminded her that they had visited this temple the first time when they moved to Chicago though they never knew that it was the Visa temple of Sai Baba. That time they could not get darshan as it was closed. Thereafter considering that the temple was closed forever, they never went back there. Her last visit to the closed door was 3 years back in 2019. Now they called up the temple and found it to be open. Anu's joy knew no bounds. They were told to enter the temple from the back door as the main entrance was always locked (no wonder they could not go inside the temple the first time they went). Anu reached the temple with a pounding heart as Baba had already given her the desired signal. Her heart could sense the Leela of Sai behind calling them in that Visa temple. On enquiry they found that Pandit ji (priest) was not there then, but a volunteer got her connected to him on a phone call. She told pandit ji that they got to know that it was the Visa temple of Sai Baba and they came there to pray for their US visa extension. Pandit Ji's words were the sweetest words she had listened to in a long time. He told her not to worry at all, and that with Sai's grace, their US visa would definitely get extended.

Anu continues narrating

'This was music to my ears, and a definite sign from Sai as I had been constantly asking Him for one.'

Pandit ji tried to allay all her fears and asked her to leave her details in the temple so that he could connect with her and perform a pooja (worship) coming Thursday. Pandit ji called her on Tuesday, May 17, 2022, and after listening to her story advised her along with her husband to do a Saaptaahik Parayan of Shri Sai Satcharita (week-long reading of Shri Sai Satcharita) starting Thursday, May 19, 2022. He explained the entire vidhi (procedure) of doing the Parayan, and asked them to completely surrender to Sai.

On the evening of Thursday, May 19, 2022, both of them started the Parayan. Her husband was still trying his last bit and had set up some time with a senior colleague, the next day, Friday. The colleague had been helping him meet new people for prospective roles. Since less than three weeks were left now, her husband wanted to update his colleague that nothing had worked out so far, and still thank him for his support and guidance all along. His colleague mentioned that he wanted him to touch base with another senior colleague in the organisation regarding a role offering in their department. Anu's husband tried to get in touch with the other colleague but got to know that he was on a vacation till the end of May 2022. It was a race against time, with their flying date back to India (June 8, 2022) just around the corner.

Anu and her family had less than 3 weeks left and for a role to work out and visa documentation to be prepared, it would normally take more than a month. Her husband tried connecting with the other colleague's assistant and explained the whole situation. She was truly *'Sai-Sent'* as she got his interview scheduled with the other colleague, who was on leave, on Monday, the fifth day of the paraayan. The interview went well and the other colleague now wanted him to meet up with four more colleagues. This would have easily taken about two weeks, given their seniority but the assistant helped again in scheduling time with them over the next 3-4 days. They continued their Shri Sai Satcharita Saaptaahik Paraayan with complete devotion and surrender to Sai's will and completed it on Wednesday, May 25, 2022. Thereafter they donated food the next day i.e. Thursday. Her husband got confirmation on Friday, May 27, 2022, that all his interviews had gone off very well, and he had been confirmed in the new role.

This was news they had been waiting to hear for so long, and Sai answered all their prayers filling them with immense gratitude for Him. By His grace, the immigration team prepared their US visa renewal documentation at record speed. The application for renewal was submitted on June 8, 2022, the day they were scheduled to fly back to India, just one day prior to the expiry of their US visas. Sai kept showering them with HIS kindness and generosity as the new role offered was remote, and her husband could work from anywhere in the USA. So they moved to the city where their elder daughter attended University to be with her.

There are no words to express the deep reverence Anu and her family has developed for Sai, and no amount of gratitude they express is enough. HE is truly a miracle-maker and has filled their lives with *'His infinite Kripa'* (grace). Sai has also blessed this move of theirs by coming in Anu's dreams several times, and they have offered their thanks to Him countless times.

Anu's message to devotees ...

> Follow His two cardinal principles of 'Shraddha and Saburi' (Faith and Patience), and completely surrender to Him. He will sail you through all the obstacles in your life.

May Sai be with you, always!

Anu Malhotra

USA
Email : malhotranu@yahoo.co.in

29

FAITH INSTILLED

If any devotee meditated on him day and night with complete self-surrender, he experienced complete union with Him like sweetness and sugar, waves and sea, eye and its sight.
Chapter XIX– Shri Sai Satcharita

It was in the beginning of 2019 when day and night, in subconscious state of mind, Shabana started perceiving the idol of an old man in the middle of a holy place, appearing so merciful and pious. Her life was miserable that time, but the supreme divinity in that idol made her restless to chase the power, to worship and merge in it, forgetting everything. The realisation that this bond was not just a new but of infinite beginning of life increased her curiosity to find HIM out and Baba himself unfolded His identity in no time. Thus, her never-ending journey with her Sai Baba started. As soon as she found him, Baba appeared before her with his Sagun form for the first time on the way when she was bound for an exam, and allowed Shabana to experience the supreme bliss of meeting him.

Once Baba entered, her good fortune started experiencing Baba's grace in the form of miracles. That phase of her life was stormy and it was Progya P Ganguly ji who helped her to get Baba's Udi through Sir Sujay Khandelwal ji, which enabled her to establish a beautiful connection with all the pure souls devout to Baba, also brought about new lights to overcome the ebb and flow. Since then, Baba has been holding her hand with all his motherly love and power to get through adversity, making the path easy and enjoyable one, concurrently awakening and improving spirituality in her by reading of Shri Sai Satcharita.

Shabana narrates...

'Baba showed his presence everywhere whenever I sought it, sometimes even without being asked. I feel myself blessed enough to share some of the wonderful incidents that happened to me.'

The proximity of Baba generated new hope to start all over again with her work at the time when she was stuck and surrounded by difficulties of life, she had lost her form and all the hope to continue.

She was in the middle of her PhD and under Baba's shadow she started again. She got the last chance for field work amid COVID-19. Miracles started happening every single day throughout the period. In fact, Baba confirmed his presence during her field visits by letting her see His picture at an unexpected place inhabited by indigenous and guided her on the right path for a fruitful sample collection for her work, and to her surprise make her way when lost in the dense forest, arranged vehicle for her in the late evening where there was no hope of getting one by that time.

With Baba's grace, she headed to the next phase of the work. She had to get the analysis done at some other institutions as soon as possible. But it was so unfortunate that she got high fever all of a sudden just before she started the work, eventually leading to chickenpox by next day. It was so painful and within few days she got lesions all over her face and body. She had to stop where she was and out of anxiety and depression she was about to quit. Then she started interrogating Baba about her fault. She cried every day and prayed for his mercy. She asked for his Udi and got it through Yokesh Gawtham ji. Gradually her health condition improved, and wonder of wonders happened that the scars started leaving her face so rapidly which was beyond anyone's expectation.

Baba turned impossible into possible and finally she got her analysis done without any further hindrance. Baba listened to her prayers and showed lots of miracles during the entire analysis period, comforted her with a better stay, cooperation from the right people and financial support. The confidence and faith Baba provides to his devotees is so phenomenal.

Shabana narrates...

May Baba always shape me to become the best version of myself as a human being.

Jai Sai Ram

Shabana Hassan
Diphu, Karbi Anglong, Assam
Mob : (+91) 6000791313
Email : shabanah28@gmail.com

30

LAMP OF FAITH

Baba said to Megha - 'I require no door to enter. I have no form nor any extension; I always live everywhere. I carry on, as a wirepuller, all the actions of the man who trusts Me and merges in Me.' Baba confirmed his faith. Chapter XXVIII - Shri Sai Satcharita

Baba pulled Ajita towards him in 2012. Since then, HE started coming in her dreams. He healed her when she was sick, He took Dakshina from her, He comforted her when she felt insecure. She started doing 9 weeks Sai Vrat where Baba started fulfilling her small wishes. She felt HIS presence in her life as He started taking care of her family.

Once while she was lying down in her bed, suddenly she felt a hand on her head. On a reflex she opened her eyes and turned around to see who it was.

To her surprise there wasn't anyone. Then her eyes felt on the table calendar which was placed on her bed side table. It was just a fraction of a second and if anyone was around couldn't move out of her room so quickly. Confused she gazed at Baba's picture in the calendar and asked Baba was this you? Baba's silence even spoke that,

'Yes, It Was Me.'

In 2020, Ajita started doing Parayan (reading Shri Sai Satcharita). She felt his strong presence when she started doing Parayan. She got a beautiful statue which came all the way from Shirdi and she felt again that Baba is there for her. On first Thursday of her Parayan she was very happy and excited that she is going to do something which she wanted to do for a long time. She got rose and marigold flowers for Baba and with full devotion she read her allotted chapters lighting up a Diya. After Parayan, she clicked a photo, zoomed it and to her surprise she could see Baba on rose petals. She felt so blessed and her happiness knew no bounds. On 2nd Thursday of her Parayan, Baba again appeared on a photo which was so clear and on 3rd Thursday of Parayan Baba appeared on a Banana and on 4th Thursday she received Shri Sai Satcharita from an anonymous person. These were the days which built up unconditional faith in Ajita, for Sai Baba. Now her day starts with Sai. She spends

3 hours on an average doing pooja of Sai and her day ends with Sai. Now she has become a staunch devotee of Sai.

Earlier, Ajita had been for a day trip to Shirdi twice, but in the month of May 2022, Baba called her to Shirdi for 3 days. During this visit Baba gave her the opportunity to see the Aartis which she hadn't experienced earlier because of her short visits. Her husband got an opportunity to hold the Palki in a Sai Sandhya. Her immense faith and devotion grown in the recent years was complimented during this visit as she got the fruits in terms of unlimited bliss from Baba in Shirdi. Content and happy she returned to Delhi.

It was 24 October, 2022, the day of Diwali. She was super busy arranging house for the festivities. Hence, she completely forgot to buy Diyas for the house. When she realised the same it was too late to go to the market. After thorough searching she found a tea candle. Tea candles are generally very small made of wax and they do not light for more than 2-3 hours. Looking at it she cursed her memory for not remembering to buy Diyas as she wanted her house lit for the entire Diwali night. Anyway, she lit the tea candle in front of Baba and prayed that it should burn its maximum and she went to sleep. When she woke up in the morning at 6.00 o'clock and went to see Baba, which is her daily routine for long now. To her surprise she saw that the small candle was still burning. She immediately understood Baba's Leela. She remembered the story from Satcharita how Baba had once lit the Diyas with water. Tears of gratitude went down her cheeks. She thanked Baba once again for fulfilling her wish. Baba is omnipresent and omniscient. He knows and gives without asking what His bhakta's wants and He fulfills them at the right moment.

Ajitha Tripathy
Delhi
Mob : (+91) 9868701230

31

AND MAMA RETURNED

Sapatnekar was surprised to see that the story which Baba related was his own, and he wondered how Baba knew every detail of it. He came to know that He was omniscient and knew the hearts of all. When this thought crossed his mind, Baba still addressing the shepherdess and pointing to Sapatnekar said - fellow blames Me and charges Me with killing his son. Do I kill people's children? Why does this fellow come to the Masjid and cry? Now I will do this I will again bring that very child back in his wife's womb. With these words He placed His blessing and on his head and comforted him saying - feet are old and holy, you are care-free now; place entire faith in Me and you will soon get your object. Chapter XLVIII - Shri Sai Satcharita

In 2015 January Rajyashree, who used to reside in Kolkata, India moved to USA. Till then She didn't know Who Sai Baba was. She didn't hear or know about Baba from her childhood but got to know about him when she left India. There she attended several Pooja and bhajans and got acquainted with Shree Sai Baba. Such are ways of our Baba to connect to his devotees. One day her Didi, Suchi Didi, who was about to leave from USA gifted her a small idol of Sai Baba as a parting gift which she had herself brought from Shirdi. There comes Baba in her house.

In 2016 she came to India for a short visit and during that visit she came to know about the illness of her Mama (Maternal Uncle) who was very dear to her. She met him and spent quality time with him but ultimately, she had to return back to America. After returning from India on 25th December that year, she got the breaking news that her Mama had left for heavenly abode. She was completely shattered by the news as she used to regard him as her father figure and being all alone abroad she felt more miserable and depressed.

After this incident one day an ardent devotee of Sai Baba, named Anjuli Khare who happened to live beneath in her apartment gave her Shri Sai Satcharita and the miracle was that it was in her mother tongue Bengali. Anjuli had gone to the temple there and surprisingly it was the last copy of Satcharita in Bengali left there which she gave her. Surprising thing is the whole episode to get a copy of Sai Satcharita that too in a Bengali (Indian Regional language) there in USA.

Anjuli knowing how depressed she was with the loss of her Mama, suggested her to do Sai Vrat for 7 days and ask Sai Baba to return her Mama back. Anjuli further said that her Mama will come back to her in the form of a child. So going by Anjuli's advise she whole heartedly and with full faith completed the 7 days of Pooja and to her pleasant surprise and by divine grace she conceived a child just 7 days after she completed the Sai Vrat Pooja. Anjuli's words were coming true and later when she sit back and thought about that incident, she firmly believed that it was Baba who made her say all so confidently and no one else.

On 12 November, 2017, she was blessed with a son. On that day like normally all new born babies cry he was also crying and when his crying didn't stop for quite some time, they all were wondering about what could be done. Then her Mami came next to her son's bed and asked 'Are you my Babun? Have you come back' (Her Mami used to call his Mama by name Babun). It is unbelievable that her son stopped crying immediately and was staring at Mami who completely believed that it was the return of Mama in the form of a child. New born babies can hardly open their eyes and her son was staring at Mami and they all watched the Miracle in complete silence and agreement of the Miracle of Sai Baba.

This was biggest Miracle of Shri Sai Baba that He returned the beloved mama in form of her child

Om Sai Ram

Rajyasree Majumdar

Kolkata

Email : rajyasreemajumdar@gmail.com

32

REKHA'S NIGHTMARE AVERTED

Wonderful Vision :- The complete story of Bhajan Mandali of Madras:

1. Devotion of Wife

2. Egoistic nature of husband 'How Baba' changed the nature of husband by wonderful vision. Chapter XXIX – Shri Sai Satcharita

Tears rolled out of Rekha's eyes as she cleaned the soiled vessels in her employer's house. She caressed the wound on her right ankle, which stood as a testimony to the atrocity of her husband. The sobs were unhindered and it looked as if she did not realise that, she was loud enough that her employer Hima heard her.

'Rekha, what makes you cry in my house on a Monday morning? Don't you know I don't like anyone shedding tears while I am performing my pooja?' Hima was visibly upset.' I always believe in starting the day on a positive note. You tell me what your problem is or please stop crying. If the solution to your problem is within my reach, let me see how I can help you' said Hima, anticipating Rekha might ask her for some monetary help. Rekha settled down with the hot cup of masala tea served by her Didi. Hima sat next to Rekha as they helped themselves with their morning tea.

'Didi see this ...' said Rekha as she showed her wound to her madam. Hima stood up with a jerk and in a state of shock, she felt a sense of guilt as she saw Rekha's swollen red ankle 'Probably, the pain made her cry. I should have been a little more sensitive' thought Hima.

'What happened Rekha?

What wounded you so badly?

Why didn't you tell me earlier?

I could have done those vessels myself' said Hima.

'No Didi, I am now used to bearing the pains that are physical and visible. They don't bother me anymore.' said Rekha 'My husband came home drunk yesterday night and hit me with the belan (rolling pin) who do I share my agony with Didi? My parents are very old, I do not want to bother them with my agony' sobbed Rekha.

'Why did you not tell me this earlier Rekha? Do you know he can be jailed for domestic violence? Come with me to the police station. Let us go right now and lodge a complaint.' Hima was angry and upset. She did not even bother to finish her tea.

'No Didi' exclaimed Rekha 'My neighbours and relatives will all shun me if I go against my husband. I will never do it Didi.' This shocked Hima all the more 'We are living in which century?' she wondered. She was taken aback with Rekha's attitude. 'You people will never learn.' Hima tried her level best to coax and cajole Rekha, but Rekha would just not agree.

Hima spent that entire night tossing and turning in her bed. The plight of Rekha was not allowing her to get even a wink of sleep. She turned around to switch on the light and get a gulp of water. The Baba's picture on her side table seemed to smile at her. 'Why did this not strike to me earlier?' she wondered. In the next 10 minutes Hima slipped into deep sleep.

Next morning, as her husband left for work, Hima hurriedly set out to bring an idol and a picture of Baba which she intended to give Rekha. 'Didi, I am here' said Rekha, as she reported to the day's work. 'Rekha, take Baba home with you today. My gut feeling says that he will set right your life' said Hima, as she handed the idol and picture of Baba to Rekha. Rekha had seen her Didi offering flowers to her Guru and doing aarti to him every single day since she joined Hima, as a house help, 5 years ago. But Rekha had her own apprehensions and was a bit skeptical in taking Him to her own house.

'Didi, I am a poor lady working in 3-4 houses to make both ends meet.' Rekha expressed her doubts 'What if I don't have anything to offer as prasad to Baba someday?' 'Rekha, have complete trust and belief in Baba and surrender to him' said Hima 'all Baba asks from his devotees, is a lot of faith and love. He infact loves his poor devotees more than the rich ones' said Hima, trying to build some confidence in her maid. Rekha was finally convinced and that day after work she took Baba home with great love and devotion.

That night Hima flew to America to be with her son for 6 months. After her return from America, Hima waited impatiently for Rekha. The locked house needed to be cleaned up and Hima was getting more and more anxious by the minute.

'Didi' she could hear the voice of Rekha at her doorstep. It sounded livelier than ever. As Hima opened the door, she was pleasantly surprised to see Rekha standing in front of her clad in a new dress and looking healthier and happier. The moment she saw her Didi, Rekha embraced her in a warm hug and minutes later too, she could feel Rekha clasping her tightly and not wanting to let go of her Didi.

'Didi, now I believe in the saying God-Sent. You truly are God sent to me' she said 'from the day I took Baba home, my drunkard husband completely gave up alcohol Didi. He does not hit or scold me anymore, and guess what Didi, he had not allowed my parents to enter our house for the last 20 years. Now, they happily visit us. If I am away at work and they come home, he himself makes coffee for them Didi. Last 20 years, he had not asked them if they needed a glass of water also.' Rekha had tears of joy flowing from her eyes.

Hima's throat chocked with emotions, when she thought how Baba had turned around a husband and wife's sour relationship of 20 years in just 6 months. She mentally bowed to her Guru.

'Didi, my only wish now is to visit him in Shirdi and you have to book my bus tickets for that trip' continued a happily chattering Rekha. 'If Baba is willing, so be it' said Hima as they both headed to clean their pooja room and light a lamp to her Baba.

Om Sai Ram

Anonymous Devotee

33

BABA MAIN JAAOON ?

Shirdi is midway between and equidistant from Rahata on one side (south) and Nimgaon on the other (north). Baba never went beyond these places during His life time. He never saw any railway train nor travelled by it. Still, He knew exactly the timing of arrival and departure of all trains. Devotees who acted according to Baba's instructions (re: their departure) which were given by him at the time of taking His leave fared well, while those who disregarded them suffered many a mishap and accident. Chapter VIII – Shri Sai Satcharita

Anupama was born in a small town in Punjab. She completed her schooling from Rajasthan. Later, she moved to Chandigarh with her parents and siblings.

In the year 2000, soon after getting married, she migrated to Australia with her husband. Since her childhood, Anupama had millions of questions related to God, suffering, death, karma, religion, rituals etc. She understood at very young age that she is not exactly religious but has extreme thirst for spirituality. She definitely believed in that One Supreme power above controlling this whole Universe, Cosmos with such perfection.

Apart from minor ups and downs in life, things were going fine. But around 2005 due to some family crises everything started crumbling down drastically with each passing day. In 2010, on insist of her family and friends she tried worshipping various deities' or forms of Gods but her heart was ever thirsty for peace. Nothing worked. Deep down in her heart her search for God had begun! She didn't know where she was being pulled away with the emotional challenges in her life. This is the time when any human being needs a God in the form of a true guide or Guru. After all, Guru is God! *(Gurur Brahma Gurur Vishnu).*

In 2010, she visited India and had put up at her in-laws place in Delhi. There one day while they were relaxing in their living area, the doorbell rang. Her husband got up and opened the door and found a Fakir Baba standing at the door. Her husband started talking to him. Anupama had a quick peek outside to see who was there. She just noticed that the fakir had a very overpowering aura and red eyes and also a little photo of Shirdi Sai Baba in his kamandal (earthen pot). That's all she noticed, not paying much heed to the sadhu as she thought there are plenty of such fakirs roaming in the streets begging money or dakshina. Upon asking her husband what the fakir was saying he said that the fakir told him lot of things from his past, his present situation and also his future and surprisingly everything correct. Later during this trip, she went to her parent's home in Chandigarh. During that time one day along with her husband she went to see a relative from her husband's side. As soon as she stepped in their house, she was instantly frozen and wonderstruck as if engulfed with some powerful divine light! She saw beautiful big pictures of Sai Baba hanging everywhere in their house smiling on her. As if waiting for her. She felt a realm of awakening amidst the hunt of a Guru. She felt as if she had got everything in life then. She felt her eyes were moist out of so much divine bliss that she was experiencing. No words can express this but the feeling was something like meeting a long-lost best friend or like meeting one's mother after years of separation. But here she perhaps found everything, her Universe in the form of Shirdi Sai Baba, her Guru, her God from many previous births. Anupama's heart was shouting out

'Oh! I found you...I know you...we have met before many times!

Aap hi ko toh mai dhundh rahi thi.. where were you Sai?'

You were the one whom I was looking for.

Clearly the host family were Sai devotees.

Anyway, the same day before dinner the host family took her and her husband to a Sai temple nearby. The temple had a Dwarkamai upstairs where she surrendered and prayed with heavy heart and asked for something impossible to resolve. And believe it or not the very next day the prayer was instantly answered. No, it was not coincidence but she could clearly sense Baba pulling her and taking her into HIS fold. Anupama was now sure she had knocked the right door which she was looking for. She started connecting to him or rather Sai started pulling her. And since then, her life is full of unbelievable Sai miracles or leelas. She started getting closer to Sai and gradually HE started sorting all her crisis in his own ways.

Baba called Anupama to Shirdi first time in 2015 along with her husband and son and there after twice more from 2015-22. Her bond and relationship with Baba became stronger and stronger each passing day. Since Baba chose her as His daughter, he literally washed away her sanchit (accumulated) painful karmas and brought huge transformation in her higher consciousness.

In 2022 suddenly something beautiful and unimaginable happened in her life. This time Baba called her all alone from Australia to Shirdi to stay for one whole month with Him in Shirdi. It was her dream come true as in her previous Shirdi visits she could stay hardly two days along with her family. And just note the date when she was called to Shirdi, Mother's Day, 8 May, 2022. No, it cannot be a coincidence. When Baba enters our life everything is actively planned and steered by Him. Yes, Sai Ma called Anupama on Mother's Day to shower her with Her motherly love and give her solace and healing in Her warm lap.

As soon as she reached Shirdi she went to Dwarkamai with a bouquet to wish Sai Ma Happy Mother's Day! Throughout her stay in Shirdi she experienced innumerable enriching experiences, miracles, prayers being answered, prophetic visions. But what happened on the last day of her stay is something she can never forget throughout her life!

It was almost a month and it was her last night in Shirdi. Next day, morning 11:00 am she had to return back home to Australia via Mumbai. That day she didn't sleep whole night which is obvious. All she wanted was to sit and talk endlessly with her Sai Maa, Baba Sai and reflect on whole Shirdi pilgrimage. She finished with her packing and every day diary writing ritual. She looked at her watch, it was nearly 1:00 am at night. It was so quiet and peaceful. Just her, Baba and the sound of ceiling fan. Finally, after all was done, she sat down relaxed with her Baba's beautiful, framed picture right next to her. It was gifted to her by one of her Sai brothers in Shirdi. She sat pondering on her Shirdi trip, marveling at Sai Baba's powers, His immense love and impeccable planning for His devotees. She meditated at Baba's divine form in the picture and got lost. It was like her Guru too was waiting to sit with her and talk endlessly. She literally went into trance with tears of Guru bhakti starting to drop from her eyes. Every cell of her body could feel Baba's presence in the room so strongly. He was right there, more alive than alive people, sitting and listening. She and Baba perhaps talked million things in a second and understood even more but without a single word uttered from mouth. Suddenly, she came back to her physical realm and checked her phone to see the time. She also checked her WhatsApp and YouTube to see if Baba had any message for her. And yes, as usual He did. She randomly played a YouTube video (Video-Meeting Mahavatar Babaji. Babaji's message to all from the land of Himalayas). As She played the video, she was absolutely shocked. The whole ocean seemed overflowing from her eyes in the form of divine tears. Because the video conveyed exactly what she was experiencing that time. It was about a devotee of another ascendent master, who once had clear darshan of his Guru in the Himalayas at 'Kedarnath'. And the way he was expressing his love for his Guru made her feel, her Guru's presence even stronger. He narrated that his Guru carried old, frail pilgrims on His back to Kedarnath. He narrated the message his Guru imparted to an old pilgrim that he was carrying on his back to Kedarnath. Her eyes were closed and all soaked but her ears were very alert and receiving every spiritual download happening that time. True, all ascendent master are One. She could feel the message coming for her from Sai Baba through this video of Mahavatar Babaji. Just like a mother imparting a precious treasure of wisdom to her daughter before she leaves.

At the near end of the video was the treasure hidden. The message was, 'Start praying for others from your heart and soul and you will not have to pray for yourself' And what she heard next gave her chills. The message continued that even after you reach home (she was going home) keep praying for people. Get a diary, (which she had recently bought from Samadhi mandir) and write names of people who are in pain and pray for them every morning and night. Which she did now and she did see a gradual positive difference in her life and also in the lives of people she prayed for. The video finished and for some time she stayed silent with closed bedewed eyes in meditation. It was 3:30 am. The Brahmamuhurat time. She was in a non-dual state of consciousness. State of Oneness with Sai Baba and Mahavtar Babaji and literally everything around her.

After all there is only one Brahma. There is no many-ness.

This experience kind of left her so spiritually charged. Everything around her looked so new including herself. Even though she hadn't slept whole night, it must be 5 am then when she quickly recorded her whole night's experience in an audio file.

Then she took her shower, got ready to meet Baba in the Samadhi mandir to seek his blessings, permission before she leaves. She picked up Baba's picture that she was talking to whole night, with her to Samadhi mandir, Dattatrey temple, Dwarkamai, Hanuman temple and in the end to Chavadi. Everywhere she went and kept asking Baba (not in her mind but literally by speaking out), *'Baba main jaaoon?'* ('Shall I leave Baba?'), in Dwarkamai, *'Baba main jaaoon?'*, Her last spot was Chavadi, *'Baba main jaoon?'*

As soon as she was coming out of Chavadi, holding Baba's picture in her hand, an old lady stopped her. She was bit skinny, fair, short but very active Amma (old lady) with the most bright aura she have ever seen and such cheerful smile on her countenance, holding a long satka (stick), wearing a dhoti style saree and Chandan (sandal wood paste) tikka on her forehead. She talked very fast, with both her hands up in boon bestowing position said

Oh meri bachhi, meri pyari, oh Baba ki deewani, main toh tere ko sadiyon se jaanti hun. Main sab jageh par hun. Bahut jageh par mili hun main tujh se. Tere ko Kedarnath main kal dekha

Oh my sweet child, who is madly in love with Baba, I know you for ages. I am omnipresent everywhere. I have met you many a times at many places. Yesterday I saw you in Kedarnath

This rings a bell? video last night.

Along with that Amma bestowed lot of blessings upon her. Anupama felt a great pull towards her even before she spoke. As if she knew her from many past births. She felt like hugging her but she was holding Baba's picture in her hands. But she bowed down to touch her feet as a mark of respect and Amma poured her abundant blessings upon her with such a broad divine smile. She had never been to Kedarnath but Masters willing one day she will. She stayed in Shirdi whole month but had never ever seen or met her. Then while entering Chavadi she said, *'Aur koi sewa ho to batana aur Theek Se Jaana.'* She immediately stopped there with gooseflesh and went speechless and blank. Baba finally answered that Yes, my child you can go and take care. She hugged Baba's picture that she was holding and bowed her head to Chavadi and went back to her hotel to depart.

How beautiful is that! Both God and His devotee only crave for each other's bhaav (affection) and strong faith/trust. That's all is needed to realise and connect with God. A Guru (God) and His devotee always recognize each other when there is pure love and devotion oozing between them. They manifest for each other, come running for each other immediately whenever called with pure love and devotion.

Anupama Khanna Arora
Australia
Email : brighteye.007@yahoo.com

34

BIRTH OF SHRADDHA

One, Gopalrao Gund, was a Circle Inspector at Kopergaon. He was a great devotee of Baba. He had three wives, but had no issue. With Sai Baba s blessings, a son was born to him. In the joy that he felt regarding the event, an idea of celebrating a fair or 'Urus'1 occurred to him in the year 1897, and he placed it for consideration before other Shirdi devotees, viz. Tatya Patil, Dada Kote Patil and Madhavrao Deshpande (Shama). They all approved of the idea, and got Sai Baba s permission and blessings. Chapter VI – Shri Sai Satcharita

Sowmya was more than relieved when her mother Mangala picked up her call.

'Hello beta, Are you already back from your Chennai trip? You had told me you would be returning only tomorrow.' Mangala tried to hide the disappointment in her tone. Her daughter and son in-law were both extremely busy, practicing dentists and she knew how important a holiday break was for them.'

'No mom! We aren't back yet.' replied Sowmya. 'I am calling you as I sit on bench in the Mahabalipuram beach. I just witnessed an interesting incident, that I was eager to share with you mom'. replied Sowmya.

'Go ahead my child' said Mangala, as she was all ears to listen to her daughter.

'Mom, I and Nilesh stepped out for an evening stroll. Barely about 10 minutes into our walk, I noticed an old man following us. I was quite scared, when I observed him for a few minutes. It was quite evident that he was following us and not headed elsewhere. Sharing my apprehension with Nilesh, both of us decided to sit down on the bench nearby. If the old man was not following us and rather headed in the same way, he would simply walk ahead of us. Nilesh agreed and we sat down on a bench nearby. To my surprise, the old man settled down on the bench next to ours.' continued Sowmya. 'Both of us, tried to keep our composure and stared at the vast sea in front of us. Mom you will not believe what happened next' continued Sowmya in her excited tone.

By now, Mangala could not hold her curiosity, while her motherly instinct, worried about the safety of her beloved daughter, she was only too sure that all was well with her daughter. 'Come on! Go ahead.' said Mangala.

'The old man stared at me for a few minutes mom.' Sowmya continued.... 'He looked straight in my eyes and spoke to me mom' He told me 'You will be the witness to the best news of your life in less than a year. Come and see me after that. Until then do not eat in any death ceremony or *shradh*.'

'I was too shocked to react mom. I just nodded in agreement with due respects to his age. After a few minutes, me and Nilesh got up and continued our walk, and guess what happened next. When I turned back after a few seconds, I could not find the old man anywhere, not sure how he vanished into thin air.'

Mangala had a vague but confident smile on her face, for she knew what exactly had transpired. She had just started reading Sai Satcharita three days back, to seek blessings of Baba to bless her daughter with a child and Baba had already given his darshan!

Mangala went to her pooja room, lit a ghee diya (oil lamp) in front of her Baba and folded her hands. No words needed to be spoken. It was just that she was eternally grateful to her guru for having given darshan in the most unexpected way to her daughter!

The family was elated to hear the news of Sowmya's pregnancy. Now, slowly Sowmya connected the dots and realised who the old man was. It was not anyone other than Baba. Sowmya was blessed with a healthy girl child and she decided to name her daughter 'Shraddha'. No other name would have been more apt.

It was another Thursday morning, yet again in the same household in Mysore, Mangala offered the ghee sweet Pongal (a south Indian sweet dish) as a prasadam (offering) to Baba. 'This is week 8 of my 9-week Vrat (fasting) Baba' she pleaded with her guru 'My strong faith in you still continues.'

Weekend as usual, Mangala picked call of her son and daughter in-law Shipra, settled in Germany. 'Hello mummy' Shipra spoke in an excited tone 'Soon, you and daddy will be grandparents.' Mangala was speechless for a moment. Her guru had blessed her again and fulfilled her wish yet again. By now Mangala had lost the count of how many times Baba had blessed her and granted her whatever she prayed for. This time she had held Baba's 9-week Vrat to bless her son and daughter in law with a child and Baba blessed her yet again.

'My grandchildren are all blessings of Baba' said Mangala as she sat down with all her 3 grandchildren during a family union. She hugged them all tight and only felt the presence of Baba all around her!

Om Sai Ram

Anonymous Devotee

35

THE POSTER COMPETITION

Baba's words were always short, pithy, deep, full of meaning, efficient and well-balanced. 'Those who are fortunate and whose demerits have vanished; take to My worship.' Chapter XIII – Shri Sai Satcharita

Dr Rajashree a resident of Bengaluru has 9 long years of association with Sai Baba since 2013. During these years she has experienced many miracles. Rajashree was a curious child wanting to know more and more always. Since childhood she had visited many temples, many gods but couldn't rest herself on anyone until she met her Sai. It was in 2013 when she lost her job and struggling, then in October that year she happened to visit Shirdi for the first time.

Rajashree narrates…

As the 2nd of 11 sayings of Baba states, 'The wretched and miserable will rise to joy and happiness as soon as they climb the steps of the mosque,' I had a unique experience when I saw Baba for the first time in the Samadhi Mandir of Shirdi. Though recently I lost my job, there was no single reason for being happy, still my heart was filled with immense joy and peace when I had an eye contact with Baba. As if Baba is sitting live in front of me and a wave of electric current passed through me. That emotional state of happiness can never be expressed in words. Since then, she never had to look back and is moving forward each step, each moment with Baba. Her day starts with Baba and ends with Baba.

During her PhD, she once did Sai Saptaha Parayan for the first time. On the completion of Parayan, a miracle happened. An International Conference was held in the University and there was a poster competition among delegates in which 114 participants presented their research work. She was one among them who just decided, one day before the competition, to take part. So, it was obvious that not much preparation was done. But by the blessings of Sai, she was surprised to win the first prize in poster competition drubbing many seniors and other delegates who were much more prepared and deserving.

Rajashree narrates...

'I have prayed Baba for my sister's son, for my brother, for my friend. Miraculously Baba has answered all my prayers. I am so blessed that Baba has given me a place in his lotus feet. Each passing day my faith deepens in Him and I feel His divine presence in my life. I wish to devote my life in the service of others with grace of Lord Sai and make my life meaningful.'

Om Sai Rakshaka Sharanam Deva

Dr. Rajashree Ranjita
Bangalore
Mob : (+91) 9342195264
Email : drrajashreeyoga@gmail.com

36

SAI LEELA WITH JAYSHREE

My stories are listened to, all the diseases will be got rid of. So, hear My stories with respect; and think and meditate on them. Chapter III– Shri Sai Satcharita

Om Sai Ram

Jayashree got married in the year 1985 in Mumbai. Her mother-in-law was a staunch devotee of Sai and by virtue of this Jayashree also slowly started believing in Sai and now she herself has become a staunch Baba devotee. By the grace of Sai, she has experienced a lot of miracles in her lifetime of which few are as below...

1. Jayashree was married for 6 years and was childless. In-spite of several remedies, she did not conceive. In the year 1991 she shifted her house to Dahisar where there was a Sai temple very close

to her house. She used to visit Baba's temple every Thursday and used to pray day and night to bless her with a child. Sai heard her prayers and she got pregnant soon. When sonography was done, it was found that she had twins. Unfortunately, just one child survived, as she had a premature delivery in 1992. The survived child was hospitalized due to complications but by Baba's blessings and Grace he recovered and now her boy is 30 years old working and happily married. Sai blessed her with a daughter again in 1994.

2. In the year 2006 Jayashree along with her family travelled from Mumbai to Nagpur to attend the wedding of her niece. Her brother had put them up in a nice hotel. On the very first evening was the event of Sangeet. She attended the sangeet and came back to her room and to her surprise she saw the room open. She remembered that she had kept her jewellery box in her suitcase which she found open. Hurriedly she opened the flap of her suitcase and found the jewellery box missing. She was supposed to wear the same jewellery next evening for the wedding which was missing. Jayashree cried silently and prayed to Baba to show miracle as read in chapter 25 of Satcharita. Missing jewellery was reported to the Hotel manager. They kept searching and interrogating

all staff but couldn't find it. Finally, Baba heard her prayers and at 2 am in the night a few people came with her jewellery box asking whether that was the one missing. It was a hotel boy who out of need and greed had stolen the same and finally he confessed and the jewellery was handed over to Jayashree. She checked the box and found everything intact and thanked Baba for his Leela.

3. In 2021 during the Covid times Jayashree along with her husband was travelling back from Dubai to her home town Nagpur. Those days all international passengers were given permission to enter India after a Rapid Covid test at the airport. Mandatorily, both went through the test and to utter surprise her husband's report came positive inspite of any symptoms what-so-ever. Protocol was such that anyone who tested positive was immediately transferred to hospital until recovery. Jayashree argued with the airport authority that there were no symptoms so how can they admit him to a hospital. There was a risk in hospitalization as she had heard of many patients who got admitted in hospital but never came back home, losing their lives. Jayashree was extremely worried. She pleaded to the authority but to no avail. Then she prayed to Baba for help. While the authorities were preparing for hospitalization, Jayashree was

continuously praying to her Sai to show some miracle. All hopes lost and her husband started getting ready to go with all his bag to the hospital when suddenly a call from a person of higher authority came.

'No need to hospitalize him but isolate him for 7 days at home'

His words were music to her ears. Her heart filled with joy and her eyes out of tears of gratitude for the blessings of Sai. On further discussion that officer turned out to be a Sai devotee and then she could understand the Leela of Sai.

Jayshree Menon
Nagpur
Email : menonjayashree8@gmail.com

MIRACLES OF SAI WITH SUJAY KHANDELWAL

Miracles of Sai with Sujay Khandelwal is a channel on YouTube with its pages on Facebook & Instagram.

It was Sainath's wish that these media platforms be created & reach out to the devotees across the globe in November 2021. Since then every Thursday there is a video uploaded with a new devotee who shares his Leelas with Sai.

Since the inception, XX videos has been uploaded which has attracted devotees from across the world. Currently its growing at a rapid speed with more & more devotees, volunteering to share from across the globe.

Miracles are out of the box extraordinary pleasant happenings in our lives by divine Almighty. The Magnanimous Omnipresent Sai Baba a blessing to mankind comes to rescue of anyone who earnestly asks for help and bails him out of trouble which has happened with millions of people over several decades.

This channel endeavours to bring you first-hand experience of such Miracles by the recipient themselves so that you can relate to them easily and benefit out of it.

By the grace of Sai Samarth many people have benefited immensely over the decades and now over a century such Miracles keep happening in lives of people across the world.

Go ahead, try and connect to Baba and feel the divine experiences which can really change your life.

Om Sai Ram

SAI SANGAM

Sai Sangam started by Sujay is a collective pilgrimage to Shirdi which takes place twice in a year around April and November months. This event is popular amongst devotees from different corners of the world, here they meet and spend 3 or 4 blissful days in Shirdi with fulling all their spiritual desire and exchange glory of lord Sai. The event features starting from Prabhat Pheri to various Aarti's and Baba's Palki also. A blissful evening of Sai Bhajans by Sai Mitr group is icing on the cake. This Sai Sangam started with 75 devotees and grew to 125 devotees in just 5 months and in coming times promises to be even bigger and grand event. Devotees visit old age home, orphanage and perform functions to bring smiles to their faces and do the pious seva of Annadaan. They also visit Samadhi Mandir, Dwarkamai and lots of important religious temples nearby Shirdi.

SAI SATSANG

Sai Satsang a pure divine and blissful gathering of Sai devotees across the world takes place for an hour on Zoom platform every Saivaar (Thursday) 8 pm to 9 pm IST. Conceived and hosted by Sujay who invites Devotees across the world to share their miraculous experiences followed by melodies of Sai Bhajan by Sai Mitr volunteers. This hourly program is operated through a WhatsApp group called Shirdi Sai Satsang group which has around 350 participants who express their love and devotion towards Baba as per their likings. Satsang with Sujay is becoming popular by the day as number of participants increasing on weekly basis and express their earnest gratitude for such a unique platform.

Come & join us to experience the Bliss of the epitome of spirituality our Sadguru Shri Sainath Maharaj.

To join whatsapp on (+91) 9051155503

DWARKAMAI - A MAGICAL TRIP

The miracle of Sai Baba of Shirdi are known to one and all. We read about them in articles or hear about them from people who have experienced them first hand. It only strengthens our faith and belief in Sai Baba. But sometimes, one truly gets lucky and experienced the divine grace of Sai Baba through some magical, out of the world experiences.

The author was visiting Shirdi to find his lost connection with Sai Baba. During his visit to Shirdi, which was only for one day, the author experienced a series of such miraculous events throughout the time he was there. It did not just help him find his connect back, but also gave a new meaning and dimension to his faith in Sai Baba of Shirdi.

This book holds a best seller tag on Amazon. First edition of this book was published in 2021 and was reprinted by Sterling Publishers in 2022.

Books on
SHIRDI SAI BABA

NEW BOOKS

2020-2021

COFFEE TABLE BOOK

New Findings on Shridi Sai Baba

CHANDRABHANU SATPATHY
978 93 86245 52 6
5.5"×8.5"
222pp
Paperback ₹ 300

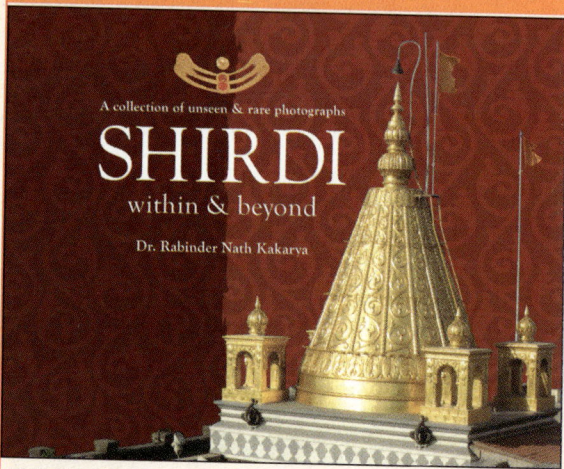

Shirdi Sai Baba is a household name in India as well as in many parts of the World today. Sterling Publishers are well known for publishing the largest number of books on Shirdi Sai, indeed far more than any other publisher. We endeavour to be comprehensive in the range of author and content. We also publish books on other saints and masters.

शिरडी साईं बाबा नवीन तथ्य

चन्द्रभानु सतपथी
978 93 86245 63 2
5.5"×8.5"
224pp
Paperback ₹ 300

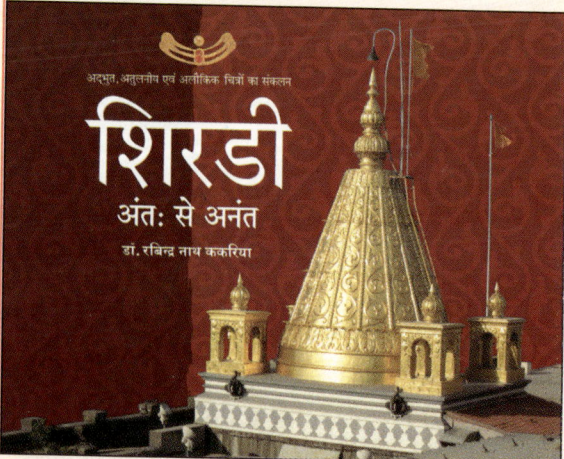

SHIRDI : within & beyond
A collection of unseen & rare photographs
Dr. Rabinder Nath Kakarya
978 81 207 7806 1   ₹ 750

शिरडी अंत: से अनंत
डॉ. रबिन्द्रनाथ ककरिया
978 81 207 8191 7
₹ 750

STERLING

mail@sterlingpublishers.in

Shri Sai Satcharita
The Life and Teachings of
Shirdi Sai Baba
Translated by Indira Kher
ISBN 978 81 207 2211 8
₹ 600(HB)
ISBN 978 81 207 2153 1
₹ 500(PB)

NEW

**Shri Shirdi Saibaba Gems
From His Philosophical
Teachings**
ISBN 978 81 944007 3 8
₹ 300

NEW

**Prema Rathna
Radhakrishnayaee**
ISBN 978 81 947772 0 5
₹ 100

NEW

Sai Musings
ISBN 978 81 950824 5 2
₹ 300

**Shirdi Sai Baba: The
Universal Master**
Sri Kaleshwar
ISBN 978 81 207 9664 5
₹ 150

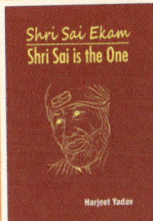

**Shri Sai Ekam
Shri Sai is the One**
Harjeet Yadav
978 93 86245 38 0
₹ 900

**Shri Sai Baba
Teachings & Philosophy**
Lt Col M B Nimbalkar
ISBN 978 81 207 2364 1
₹ 150

Shirdi Sai Baba
Anusuya Vasudevan
ISBN 978 93 86245 16 8
(64 pages plates)
₹ 200

**We need Sai forever... at 6,
16 and 60!**
Saurabh Khanna
ISBN 978 93 86245 15 1
₹ 190

**Sai Baba of Shirdi:
A Biographical Investigation**
Kevin R. D. Shepherd
ISBN 978 81 207 9901 1
₹ 450

**The Eternal Sai
Consciousness**
A. R. Nanda
ISBN 978 81 207 9043 8
₹ 200

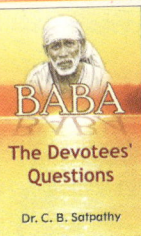

**BABA:
The Devotees' Questions**
Dr. C. B. Satpathy
ISBN 978 81 207 8966 1
₹ 150

**The Loving God:
Story of Shirdi Sai Baba**
Dr. G. R. Vijayakumar
ISBN 978 81 207 8079 8
₹ 200

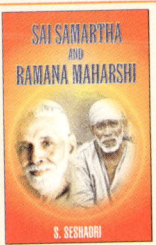

**Sai Samartha and Ramana
Maharshi**
S. Seshadri
ISBN 978 81 207 8986 9
₹150

Shri Sai Gyaneshwari
Rakesh Juneja
ISBN 978 93 86245 05 2
₹ 300

The Age of Shirdi Sai
Dr. C. B. Satpathy
ISBN 978 81 207 8700 1
₹ 300

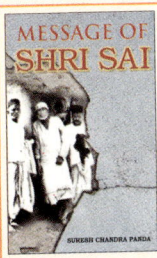

Message of Shri Sai
Suresh Chandra Panda
ISBN 978 81 207 9512 9
₹ 150

A Divine Journey with Baba
Vinny Chitluri
ISBN 978 81 207 9859 5
₹ 300

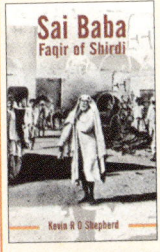

Sai Baba: Faqir of Shirdi
Kevin R.D. Shepherd
ISBN 978 93 86245 06 9
₹ 350

mail@sterlingpublishers.in

STERLING

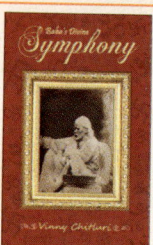
Baba's Divine Symphony
Vinny Chitluri
ISBN 978 81 207 8485 7
₹ 300

Sai Baba an Incarnation
Bela Sharma
ISBN 978 81 207 8833 6
₹ 200

Shirdi Sai Baba: The Perfect Master
Suresh Chandra Panda & Smita Panda
ISBN 978 81 207 8113 9
₹ 200

The Eternal Sai Phenomenon
A R Nanda
ISBN 978 81 207 6086 8
₹ 200

Baba's Rinanubandh
Leelas during His Sojourn in Shirdi
Compiled by Vinny Chitluri
ISBN 978 81 207 3403 6
₹ 300

Baba's Gurukul SHIRDI
Vinny Chitluri
ISBN 978 81 207 4770 8
₹ 250

Baba's Anurag
Love for His Devotees
Compiled by Vinny Chitluri
ISBN 978 81 207 5447 8
₹ 200

Baba's Vaani: His Sayings and Teachings
Compiled by Vinny Chitluri
ISBN 978 81 207 3859 1
₹ 250

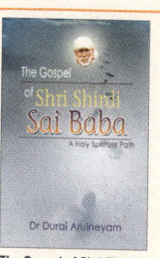
The Gospel of Shri Shirdi Sai Baba: A Holy Spiritual Path
Dr Durai Arulneyam
ISBN 978 81 207 3997 0
₹ 150

Jagat Guru: Shri Shirdi Sai Baba
Prasada Jagannadha Rao
ISBN 978 81 207 8175 7
₹ 100

Spotlight on the Sai Story
Chakor Ajgaonker
ISBN 978 81 207 4399 1
₹ 200

Shirdi Sai Baba
A Practical God
K. K. Dixit
ISBN 978 81 207 5918 3
₹ 75

Promises of Shirdi Sai Baba
(The Eleven Precious Sayings)
Bela Sharma
ISBN 978 93 85913 98 3
₹ 75

Shirdi Sai Baba
The Divine Healer
Raj Chopra
ISBN 978 81 207 4766 1
₹ 150

Shirdi Sai Baba and other Perfect Masters
C B Satpathy
ISBN 978 81 207 2384 9
₹ 200

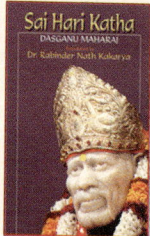
Sai Hari Katha
Dasganu Maharaj
Translated by
Dr. Rabinder Nath Kakarya
ISBN 978 81 207 3324 4
₹ 150

Unravelling the Enigma:
Shirdi Sai Baba in the light of Sufism
Marianne Warren
ISBN 978 81 207 2147 0
₹ 400

I am always with you
Lorraine Walshe-Ryan
ISBN 978 81 207 3192 9
₹ 150

BABA- May I Answer
C.B. Satpathy
ISBN 978 81 207 4594 0
₹ 150

Ek An English Musical on the Life of Shirdi Sai Baba
Usha Akella
ISBN 978 81 207 6842 0
₹ 75

STERLING

mail@sterlingpublishers.in

Sri Sai Baba
Sai Sharan Anand
Translated by V.B Kher
ISBN 978 81 207 1950 7
₹ 200

Sai Baba: His Divine Glimpses
V B Kher
ISBN 978 81 207 2291 0
₹ 95

A Diamond Necklace To: Shirdi Sai Baba
Giridhar Ari
ISBN 978 81 207 5868 1
₹ 200

Life History of Shirdi Sai Baba
Ammula Sambasiva Rao
ISBN 978 81 207 7722 4
₹ 250

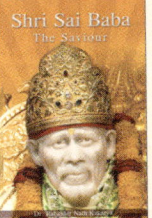
Shri Sai Baba- The Saviour
Dr. Rabinder Nath Kakarya
ISBN 978 81 207 4701 2
₹ 100

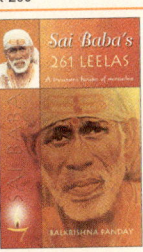
Sai Baba's 261 Leelas
Balkrishna Panday
ISBN 978 81 207 2727 4
₹ 200

A Solemn Pledge from True Tales of Shirdi Sai Baba
Dr B H Briz-Kishore
ISBN 978 81 207 2240 8
₹ 95

God Who Walked on Earth: The Life & Times of Shirdi Sai Baba
Rangaswami Parthasarathy
ISBN 978 81 207 1809 8
₹ 225

Shri Shirdi Sai Baba: His Life and Miracles
ISBN 978 81 207 2877 6
₹ 35

Shirdi Sai Baba Aratis
ISBN 978 81 207 8456 7
(English)
₹ 10

Sree Sai Charitra Darshan
Mohan Jagannath Yadav
ISBN 978 81 207 8346 1
₹ 225

The Miracles of Sai Baba
ISBN 978 81 207 5433 1 (HB)
₹ 300

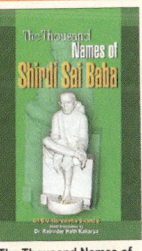
The Thousand Names of Shirdi Sai Baba
Sri B.V. Narasimha Swami Ji
Hindi translation by
Dr. Rabinder Nath Kakarya
ISBN 978 81 207 3738 9
₹ 75

108 Names of Shirdi Sai Baba
ISBN 978 81 207 3074 8
₹ 50

Shirdi Sai Speaks... Sab Ka Malik Ek
Quotes for the Day
ISBN 978 81 207 3101 1
₹ 200

DIVINE GURUS

Guru Charitra
Shree Swami Samarth
ISBN 978 81 207 3348 0
₹ 300

Sri Swami Samarth Maharaj of Akkalkot
N.S. Karandikar
ISBN 978 81 207 3445 6
₹ 250

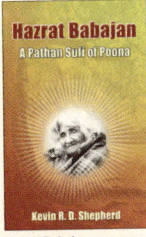
Hazrat Babajan: A Pathan Sufi of Poona
Kevin R. D. Shepherd
ISBN 978 81 207 8698 1
₹ 200

Sri Narasimha Swami Apostle of Shirdi Sai Baba
Dr. G.R. Vijayakumar
ISBN 978 81 207 4432 5
₹ 90

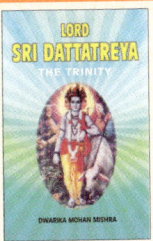
Lord Sri Dattatreya The Trinity
Dwarika Mohan Mishra
ISBN 978 81 207 5417 1
₹ 200

mail@sterlingpublishers.in

STERLING

श्री साईं सच्चरित्र
श्री शिरडी साईं बाबा की
अद्भुत जीवनी तथा उनके
अमूल्य उपदेश
गोविंद रघुनाथ दाभोलकर
(हेमाडपंत)
978 81 207 2500 3
₹ 400 (HB)

श्री साईं ज्ञानेश्वरी-महाकाव्य
राकेश जुनेजा
978 93 86245 17 5
₹ 250

हमें साईं की आवश्यकता है सदा के लिए 6, 16 और 60!
सौरभ खत्रा
978 93 86245 21 2
₹ 125

साईं ही क्यों?
राकेश जुनेजा
978 81 207 9610 2
₹ 200

जेल में साईं साक्षात्कार
राकेश जुनेजा
978 81 207 9507 5
₹ 150

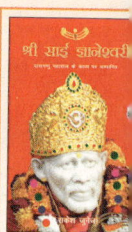

श्री साईं ज्ञानेश्वरी
राकेश जुनेजा
978 81 207 9491 7
₹ 250

शिरडी साईं बाबा के ग्यारह अनमोल वचन
बेला शर्मा
978 93 85913 97 6
₹ 75

श्री साईं चरित्र दर्शन
मोहन जगन्नाथ यादव
978 81 207 8350 8
₹ 200

साईं सुमिरन
अंजु टंडन
978 81 207 8706 3
₹ 100

बाबा की वाणी-उनके वचन तथा आदेश
बेला शर्मा
978 81 207 4745 6
₹ 100

बाबा का अनुराग
विनी चितलुरी
978 81 207 6699 0
₹ 125

बाबा का ऋणानुबंध
विनी चितलुरी
978 81 207 5998 5
₹ 150

बाबा का गुरुकुल–शिरडी
विनी चितलुरी
978 81 207 6698 3
₹ 150

बाबा-आध्यात्मिक विचार
चन्द्रभानु सतपथी
978 81 207 4627 5
₹ 175

पृथ्वी पर अवतरित भगवान शिरडी के साईं बाबा
रंगस्वामी पार्थसारथी
978 81 207 2101 2
₹ 200

साईं बाबा एक अवतार
बेला शर्मा
978 81 207 6706 5
₹ 150

साईं सत् चरित का प्रकाश
बेला शर्मा
978 81 207 7804 7
₹ 200

श्री शिरडी साईं बाबा एवं अन्य सद्गुरु
चन्द्रभानु सतपथी
978 81 207 4401 1
₹ 90

साईं शरण में
चन्द्रभानु सतपथी
978 81 207 2802 8
₹ 150

साईं – सबका मालिक
कल्पना भाकुनी
978 81 207 9886 1
₹ 200

श्री साईं बाबा के परम भक्त
डॉ. रविन्द्रनाथ ककरिया
978 81 207 2779 3
₹ 125

शिरडी अंत: से अनंत
डॉ. रविन्द्रनाथ ककरिया
978 81 207 8191 7
₹ 750

STERLING

mail@sterlingpublishers.in

 श्री साई बाबा के अनन्य भक्त डॉ. रबिन्द्र नाथ ककरिया 978 81 207 2705 2 ₹ 100	 साई का संदेश डॉ. रबिन्द्र नाथ ककरिया 978 81 207 2879 0 ₹ 200	 श्री साई बाबा के उपदेश व तत्त्वज्ञान एम. बी. निंबालकर 978 81 207 5971 8 ₹ 100	 साई भक्तानुभव डॉ. रबिन्द्रनाथ ककरिया 978 81 207 3052 6 ₹ 125	 मुक्तिदाता - श्री साई बाबा डॉ. रबिन्द्रनाथ ककरिया 978 81 207 2778 6 ₹ 65	 साई दत्तावधूता राजेन्द्र भण्डारी 978 81 207 4400 4 ₹ 75
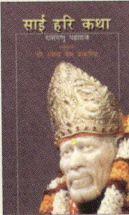 साई हरि कथा दासगणु महाराज 978 81 207 3323 7 ₹ 65	 श्री नरसिम्हा स्वामी शिरडी साई बाबा के दिव्य प्रचारक डॉ. रबिन्द्र नाथ ककरिया 978 81 207 4437 0 ₹ 100	 शिरडी साई बाबा - की सत्य कथाओं से प्राप्त - एक पावन प्रतिज्ञा प्रो. डॉ. बी.एच. ब्रिज-किशोर 978 81 207 2346 7 ₹ 95	 दिव्य भजन डॉ. रबिन्द्रनाथ ककरिया 978 81 207 9505 1 ₹ 125	 शिरडी संपूर्ण दर्शन डॉ. रबिन्द्रनाथ ककरिया 978 81 207 2312 2 ₹ 50	 शिरडी साई बाबा की दिव्य लीलाएँ डॉ. रबिन्द्र नाथ ककरिया 978 81 207 6376 0 ₹ 150
 श्री साई चालीसा 978 81 207 4773 9 ₹ 50	 शिरडी साई बाबा आरती 978 81 207 8195 5 ₹ 10	 आरती संग्रह (3D cover) on Plastic 978 81 207 8940 1 Size: 14.20 x 10.70 cm ₹ 60	 आरती संग्रह (Index Boardbook) Gold/Silver Cover ISBN 978 81 207 9057 5 Size: 10.70 x 15.45 cm ₹ 100	 आरती संग्रह (Boardbook) Green Cover ISBN 978 81 207 4774 6 Size: 11 x 15 cm (9 Leafs) ₹ 50	 शिरडी साई के दिव्य वचन-सब का मालिक एक प्रतिदिन का विचार 978 81 207 3533 0 ₹ 200

ORIYA LANGUAGE

 ଶ୍ରୀ ସାଇ ସକରିତ୍ର (ଓଡ଼ିଆ) 978 81 207 8332 4 ₹ 350	 ସାଇ ସଂଦେଶ 978 81 207 9534 1 ₹ 100	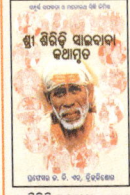 ଶ୍ରୀ ଶିରଡ଼ି ସାଇବାବା କଥାମୃତ 978 81 207 7774 3 ₹ 95	 ଶ୍ରୀ ସାଇବାବା ଉପଦେଶ ଓ ତତ୍ତ୍ୱଜ୍ଞାନ 978 81 207 9982 0 ₹125	 ଶିରଡ଼ି ସାଇ ବାବାଙ୍କ ଜୀବନ ଚରିତ (Oriya) 978 81 207 7417 9 ₹125

mail@sterlingpublishers.in

STERLING

KANNAD LANGUAGE

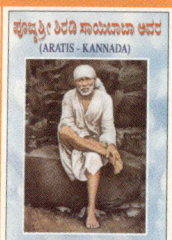
Shirdi Sai Baba Aratis
(Kannada)
₹ 10

ಬಾಬಾರವರ ಹೃದಾನುಬಂಧ
ವಿನ್ನಿ ಚಿಟ್ನೂರ್
978 81 207 9500 6
₹ 200

ಶೃಷ್ಟೀ ಶಿರಡಿ ಸಾಯಿಬಾಬಾ ಅವರ
(Kannada)
ಪ್ರೊ. ಡಾ. ಬಿ.ಎಚ್.
ಬ್ರಿಜ್-ಕಿಶೋರ್
978 81 207 2873 8
₹ 95

ಶ್ರೀ ಶಿರಡಿ ಸಾಯಿಬಾಬಾರವರ ದಿವ್ಯ ಲೀಲೆಗಳು
978 81 207 8930 2
₹ 225

ಬಾಬಾರವರೊಂದಿಗೆ ಒಂದು ದಿವ್ಯ
ಪಯಣ
ವಿನ್ನಿ ಚಿಟ್ನೂರ್
978 81 207 9975 2
₹ 200

TAMIL AND TELUGU LANGUAGE

MARATHI LANGUAGE

NEW

Life History of Sri Shirdi Sai Baba
978-93-86245-77-9
₹ 250

ஷீரடி சாயிபாபாவின் உள்ளார்த்தத்தைக்குறிக்கும் பொருள்மிகுமான வாக்குகள் (Tamil)
ப்ரொ. டா. பி.எச். ப்ரிஜ்-கிஷோர்
978 81 207 2876 9 ₹ 95

Shirdi Sai Baba Aratis
(Telugu) ₹ 10
(Tamil) ₹ 10

షిరిడీసాయిబాబా
(Telugu)
ప్రొ. డా. బి.హెచ్. బ్రిజ్-కిశోర్
978 81 207 2294 1 ₹ 95

शिर्डी साईबाबांची दिव्य वचने (Marathi)
सबका मालिक एक
दैनंदिन विचार
978 81 207 7518 3
₹ 200

THE THOUSAND NAMES OF GOD

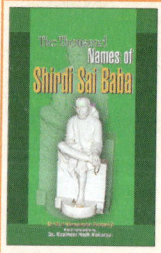
Shirdi Sai Baba
DR. RABINDER NATH KAKARYA
978 81 207 3738 9 ₹75

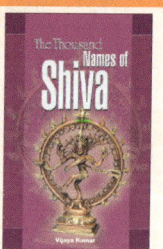
Shiva
VIJAYA KUMAR
978 81 207 3008 3 ₹75

Ganesha
VIJAYA KUMAR
978 81 207 3007 6 ₹75

Vishnu
VIJAYA KUMAR
978 81 207 3009 0 ₹75

Colouring My Way
STERLING STUDIO
978 81 207 9790 1 ₹50

108 NAMES OF GOD

Lakshmi
978 81 207 2028 2 ₹50

Shirdi Sai Baba
978 81 207 3074 8 ₹50

Durga
978 81 207 2027 5 ₹50

Shiva
978 81 207 2025 1 ₹50

Hanuman
978 81 207 2024 4 ₹50

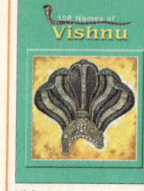
Vishnu
978 81 207 2023 7 ₹50

Sterling Publishers Private Limited
Plot No-13, Eco Tech-III, Udyog Kendra Greater Noida, Uttar Pradesh, Pin-201308 India
CIN: U22110DL1964PTC211907 GST: 09AAACS0306C1Z1
Phone No : +91 82877 98380 E-mail : mail@sterlingpublishers.in www.sterlingpublishers.in
Prices are subject to change